7MNRL

ALABAMA FOOTPRINTS Settlement

A Collection of Lost & Forgotten Stories

Read more books of the
The Alabama Footprints Series

ALABAMA FOOTPRINTS
Exploration

ALABAMA FOOTPRINTS
Settlement

More coming soon!

Additional stories of Alabama pioneers can be found on the websites:

www.alabamapioneers.com

www.daysgoneby.me

Follow on Facebook at:

http://www.facebook.com/alabamapioneers

http://www.facebook.com/daysgonebyme

and

Twitter

http://twitter.com/alabamapioneers

ALABAMA FOOTPRINTS
Settlement

A Collection of
Lost & Forgotten Stories

by

Donna R. Causey

Published by Donway Publishing

ISBN- 13: 978-1514210239

ISBN-10: 1514210231

DEDICATION

This book is dedicated to all
my friends and family in Alabama

INTRODUCTION

Before statehood, travelers to the future state of Alabama faced a formidable task as they threaded their way through the vast wilderness down paths of what was then mainly Indian country.

Until 1806, rivers and Indian trails were the only means of communication in the Alabama region, but in that year Congress provided for the construction of the first two roads. One was to connect Nashville, Tennessee, with Natchez upon the Mississippi, crossing the Tennessee River at Muscle Shoals. This road was later known as the *Natchez Trace.* The other road followed the route from Athens, Georgia, to New Orleans, passing through the settlement on the Tombigbee. It came to be known as the *Federal Road* and along it thousands of settlers later found their way to Alabama.

Prior to 1806, few trails existed in the dense forest and much labor was spent clearing a way for early settlers' wagons, pack animals and belongings. Flat boats were often used on the rivers, but even these were dangerous when unsuspected shoals or falls were encountered.

"Between the Tombigbee clearings and the settled part of Georgia lay the confederacy of the Creeks extending its boundaries northward well toward the Tennessee line. Adjoining the Creeks on the north lay the territory of the Cherokees, extending eastward into Georgia and northward into Tennessee. Between the Tombigbee and the settlements upon the lower Mississippi lay the lands of the Choctaws, and northward of them the country of the Chickasaws took in the northwestern corner of the future Alabama and extended across western Tennessee."

While many of the stories in this compilation can be found on the Alabama Pioneers website, additional information has often been provided which could not be incorporated on the website.

Visit http://alabamapioneers.com
for more unknown stories about the state of Alababama and follow on Facebook at
http://www.facebook.com/alabamapioneers
and
http://twitter.com/alabamapioneers

Table of Contents

England, France & Spain Claimed Alabama

Priest, Fur Trader And Explorer Search For The Mouth Of The Mississippi River

A priest and a fur trader from Canada seem an unlikely combination to be chosen as leaders for an expedition in search of the headwaters of the Mississippi River. However both men had specific skills which enabled them to conquer the wilds of the heart of America. Louis Joliet, the fur trader, was an experienced map maker while Father Jacques Marqette was an accompished linguist who spoke half a dozen Native American languages.

The two men set out on May 17, 1673 with five men in two birchbark canoes. They traveled down the western shores of Lake Michigan to the Fox River and on to the Wisconsin River where they stopped and carried their canoes to the Mississippi River.

After traveling about a month, the two men decided to visit an Ilinois Indian village. Leaving their crew behind to guard the canoes, they bravely walked unarmed into the village. The robes of a Jesuit priest were well-known among the Native Americans so they were welcomed by the Indians. The two men evidently made a good impression because after being fed, the chief of the village gave them a peace pipe (called a calumet) to protect them from any potentially hostile tribes. He even lent them his own ten-year-old son as a guide.

The expedition continued down the Mississippi southwardly as far as the Arkansas. Along their journey south, Marquette and Joliet talked with the local Native Americans and made maps of the region.

The calument was very useful when they passed the Ohio River, near the site of St. Louis when some Arkansas Indians became belligerent and surrounded the canoes. Marquette held the peace pipe high in the air and once it was recognized, the Indians no longer attacked them.

Still, they were unable to complete their mission. The voyage was cut short when the Quapaw Native American tribe warned them that Spanish colonials were located further south. Not wanting to risk losing the valuable information about the Mississippi River they'd acquired to the Spanish, they decided to returned to Quebec and announced the result of the exploration.

Hearing of their travels the French explorer, Robert de La Salle, organized an expedition and followed the Mississippi to the Gulf, taking formal possession of the country, April 9, 1682, in the name of King Louis XIV.

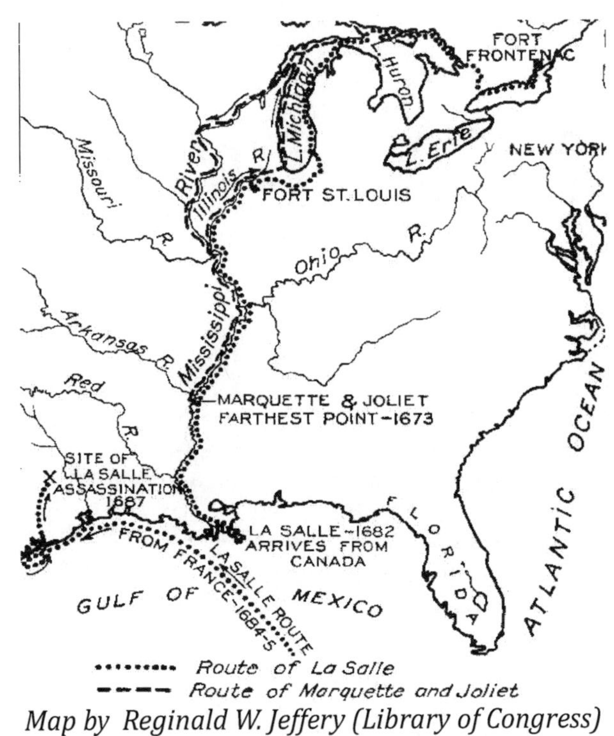

Map by Reginald W. Jeffery (Library of Congress)

Upon information by LaSalle, of his discoveries, the French government fitted out an expedition to assist him in planting a colony near the mouth of the Mississippi. They saw the importance of connecting their Canadian possessions by a chain of colonies and military posts with the Gulf of Mexico.

LaSalle's little fleet failed to find the mouth of the great river, but landed the expedition upon the coast of Texas near what is now Houston, Texas, where one ship ran aground. Some Indians started taking supplies from the wrecked ship and LaSalle's men shot at them. The men built a fort at the mouth of the Lavaca River and began to explore the area in search of the Mississippi. Most of the men died and only 8 out of 20 returned to the fort.

LaSalle and seventeen other men made a second attempt. Doubt, hardships and famine led to his murder by his own men on the headwaters of the Trinity on March 19, 1687. A few of the adventurers made their way to Canada, and the rest perished on the coast of Texas. The men who remained at the fort were killed by the Karankawa Indians.

Six years later the Canadian Iberville brothers discovered the mouth of the Mississippi and established a settlement at Biloxi. They explored the river some distance and built a fort upon the Mississippi. In 1701, Bienville broke up the establishment at Biloxi and moved the colony to Mobile Bay.

The growth of the settlements was slow and uncertain. "Fear of the savages, and of sickness from the more fertile lands of the interior, caused the colonists to hug the coast closely, and to depend for subsistence upon barter with the Native Americans and upon contributions from the home government." After ten years, only one hundred and twenty-two soldiers and one hundred and fifty-seven civilians resided in the colony.

In 1712, the King of France granted Louisiana to a wealthy speculator by the name of Crozat, who in turn sent out as governor Lamotte Cadillac to the region.

After arriving in the new land, Cadillac sent dispatches to Count Ponchartrain that Bienville's colony was "a mass of rapscallians, from Canada, a cut-throat set, without subordination, with no respect for religion, and abandoned in vice with Indian women whom they prefer to French girls."

In 1716, Bienville established a military post at Natchez, which became the nucleus for the settlement of west Mississippi. This was the only important event of the Crozat regime. In the following year his charter was annulled and Louisiana was handed over to a West India company of which John Law was the chief director.

Map United States 1717 (Library of Congress)

The story of John Law, Scottish financier and main cause of the Mississippi Bubble was related in *Alabama Footprints Book One - Exploration.* This adventure failed. The new colonists continued to hug the coast as their predecessors did and abstained from agriculture.

Finally, war accomplished what peace had failed to do. When hostilities broke out between Spain and France in 1719, the French saw the importance of strengthening the population and resources of their colony if they could save the great Mississippi from the hands of the Spainish.

France offered special inducements to settlers, and succeeded in increasing the population of the colonies very rapidly. They sent over black slaves in large numbers to cultivate rice, indigo and tobacco.

Once the hostilities ceased between Spain and France, there were many French traders settled among the Native American tribes of Alabama.

English traders from the Carolinas were becoming more common and clashes with the French traders occurred. Each tried to inflame the Native Americans against the other. French military posts extended at this time from Fort Toulouse upon the Coosa, a few miles north of Montgomery to La Harpe's Station upon Red River.

Indians complained that their peltries brought better prices from the English than from the French, and that the goods which they received from the English posts were of better quality and cheaper price than that furnished at Mobile and New Orleans. The Chickasaws and the Muscogees allied themselves with the English while the Choctaws adhered to the French. The Alabamas preserved an armed neutrality.

1755 Map by J. Hinton showing French & English settlements & Fort Toulouse as part of Georgia. (Library of Congress)

Governor Perrier, who succeeded Bienville, wrote the following in a dispatch to the home government:

> The English continued to urge their commerce into the very heart of the province. Sixty or seventy horses laden with merchandise have passed into the country of the Chickasaws, to which nation I have given orders to plunder the English of their goods, promising to recompense them by present.

In the year 1728, the province of Louisiana was guarded by 800 soldiers, and employed 2000 African slaves in labor. Her exports of indigo, cotton, tobacco, grain and lumber were becoming considerable. This growth in agriculture and trade was clouded but not checked by the Indian massacre of the Natchez settlement during the following year.

Whole Territory Of Alabama Was An Immense Wilderness

The territory of the state of Alabama was but sparsely settled in 1792, except by the natives, and they occupied only some of the principal water-courses. Fort Charlotte, at Mobile, 1792 was garrisoned with Spanish troops. The old French Tombecbe, (Tombigbee) which, in Spanish times, was called Port Confederation, contained also a Spanish garrison.

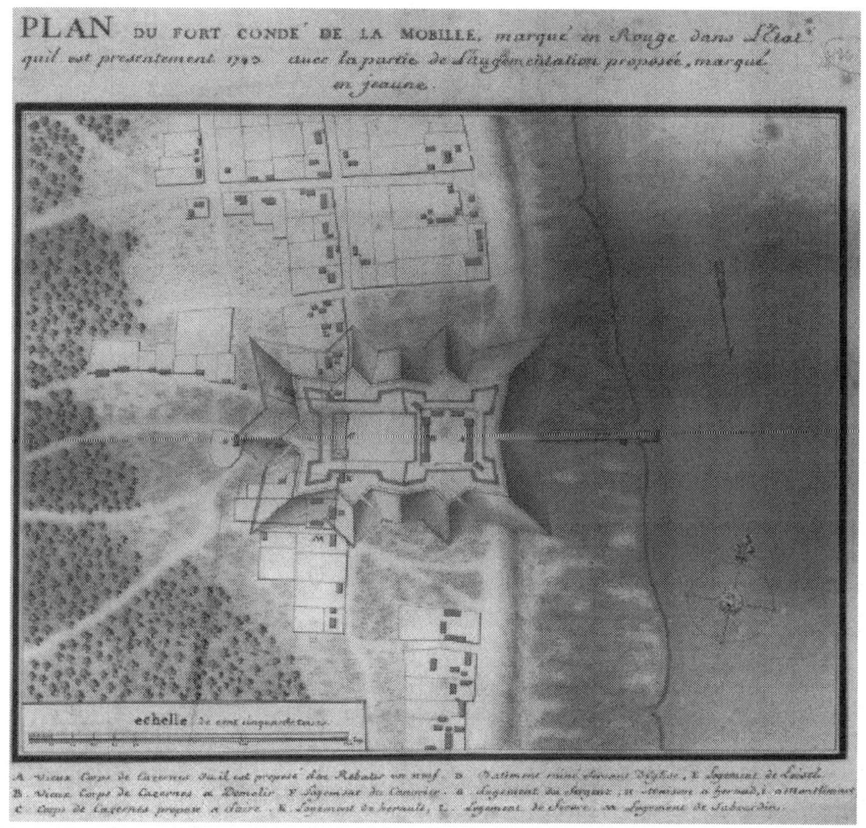

Fort Charlotte (also named Fort Conde) in Mobile, Alabama 1743 (Library of Congress)

In 1767, a colony of two hundred and nine French Protestants made a settlement upon the Escambia river north of Pensacola, Florida. They received a large grant of land from King George the III and had even been transported across the ocean at the royal expense. They built white cottages among the live oak groves, and erected a church building with one simple village spire. This colony was not long afterward desolated by the yellow fever, the scourge of the tropics.

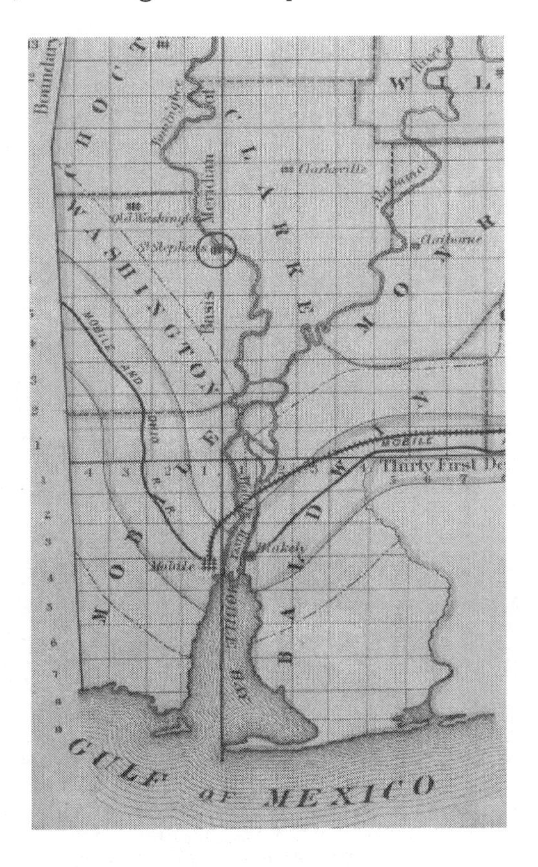

1866 Map of SE corner of Alabama where St. Stephens was located

Tensaw, an English trading post near where Stockton is located today, was repaired and occupied. A Spanish garrison occupied Fort St. Stephens, which was built upon a bluff on the Tombigbee River called by the Choctaws, Hobuckintopa. A large Spanish garrison held the fortress at Pensacola. West Florida and Louisiana were governed by the Captain-General at Havana.

The next person in authority was the Governor of Louisiana to whom all the commandants of the posts in Alabama and Mississippi were subordinate. The whole territory of Alabama was then an immense wilderness, with American trading-posts on the east upon the Oconee, and those of Spain upon the south and west, while it was uninhabited by whites as far as the distant Cumberland settlements on the north.

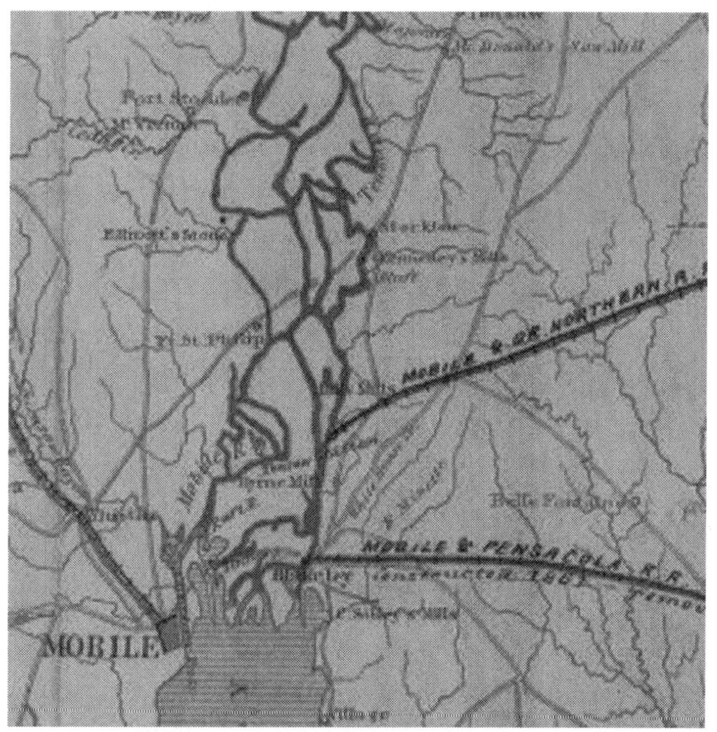

1863 map of Mobile area - Stockton and Tensaw River in SE Alabama - area of early settlement

(Library of Congress)

The most populous settlement, with the exception of Mobile, was upon the Tensaw river and lake of that name. It was composed of both whigs and royalists. The latter had been driven from Georgia and the Carolinas. Added to these, were men, *sui generis*, appropriately called old Indian countrymen, who had spent much of their lives in Indian commerce.

The most conspicuous and wealthy inhabitant of this neighborhood was Captain John Linder, a native of the Canton of Berne, in Switzerland. He resided many years in Charleston, as a British engineer and surveyor. There General McGillivray became acquainted with him, and during the revolution, assisted him in bringing his family and slaves to Alabama.

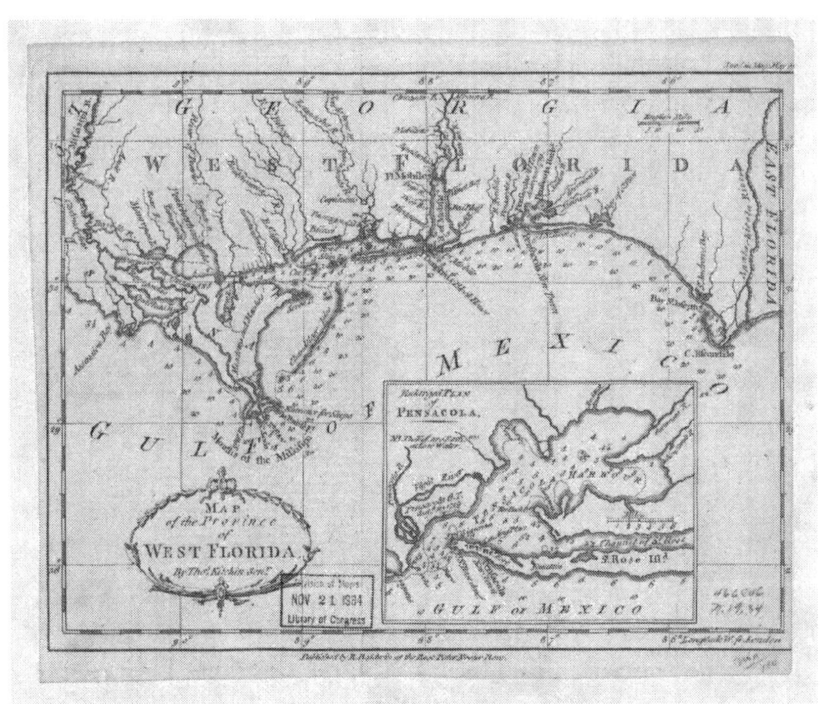

1781 map of West Florida by Thomas Kitchin

(Library of Congress)

It does not appear that in these years many additions were made to the settlers on the Mobile and Tensaw rivers. The plantations opened there must have been productive, and business enterprise was evidently not stagnant, for in 1772 the exports from Mobile and Pensacola were, according to Albert Pickett "indigo, raw-hides, corn, fine cattle, tallow, rice, pitch, bear's oil, tobacco, tar, squared timber, indigo seed, myrtle wax, cedar-posts and planks, salted wild beef, pecan nuts, cypress and pine-boards, plank of various woods, shingles, dried salt-fish, scantling, sassafras, canes, staves and heading hoops, oranges and peltry."

The cultivation of cotton had also commenced, and some small machines had been invented for separating the lint from the seed. The French planters had some machines by which, it is said by Captain Barnard Roman, in his "Florida," "seventy pounds of clear cotton can be made every day." Whitney's Cotton Gin was not invented until 1792.

Pensacola, the capital of the province, contained in 1771 about one hundred and eighty houses, which were built of wood. This, as the seat of government, was to become the first place of traffic for the coming settlers of Clarke County. The French houses of the wealthy in Mobile were of brick.

In 1775 the Thirteen United Colonies contained a population of about "three million people," extending from New Hampshire to Georgia. They were entering upon the American Revolution. West Florida did not enter this conflict so it became a secure retreat for Royalists, in the Carolinas and Georgia, who held themselves still loyal to the king of Great Britain. The banks of the Tombigbee river, then called Tombeckbee, became attractive to this large class of adventurers and refugees.

1823 Map of Alabama by John Melish with counties

(Library of Congress)

In the year 1777 an English botanist, William Bartram, visited the settled parts of West Florida. He found on the Tensaw river many well-cultivated plantations, on which settlers were then living. His route both going and coming seems to have been on the east side of the Alabama.

From him, therefore, nothing is learned concerning settlers on the west side. When near the northern boundary of the province and still beside the river, his party met with some Georgians, a man and his wife, some young children, one young woman and three young men, packing their goods on a dozen horses-who were on their way intending to settle upon the Alabama river, a few miles above its union with the Tombigbee And these "are believed" says Pickett "to have been among the first Anglo-Americans who settled in the present Baldwin county." That some such settler had already reached the Tombigbee is quite certain, so that we may safely place the commencement of what became permanent American settlement as early as the year 1777.

White settlers from other states had begun to settle on the lower Tombigbee River around 1790. They came very slowly, however, and numbered only twelve hundred and fifty souls ten years later when a census was taken. The trackless wilderness that lay between was filled with obstacles and perils that none but the boldest dared to encounter. This area in 1800 comprised the first county of the southern part of the Mississippi Territory and was named Washington. (Brewer)

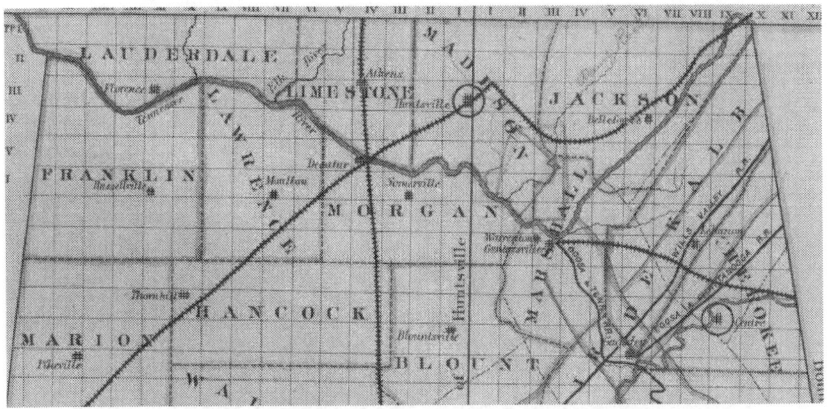

Portion of 1866 map showing counties of North Alabama

(Library Of Congress)

In 1777, some expeditionary trips by hopeful settlers through what is now Madison County occurred in north Alabama. Thomas Hutchins led a group into what was then the Indian Territory through Madison County towards Muscle Shoals. However, the Indians attacked and drove them from the area.

Colonel John Donelson led a band of some 160 persons by Madison County along the Tennessee River to settle where Nashville, Tennessee stands today. Some of the men in the party were James Cain, Isaac Neely, Benjamin Porter, John White, and John Cotton.

Joseph Martin and John Donelson, acting as agents of William Blount and Richard Caswell bought the Great Bend area of the Tennessee River from the Cherokee Indians. Griffin, Rutherford, Anthony Bledsoe and John Sevier joined Martin and Donelson in the venture.

William Blount influenced the States of Georgia and North Carolina to create Houston county, to be governed by a commission of seven men that included Martin, Donelson and Sevier. Donelson was surveyor, Sevier was Milita Colonel Commandant and Martin became Indian Agent. Wade Hampton from South Carolina joined the group venture. In total, eighty men moved into the area of Muscle Shoals and Valentine Sevier was appointed as a member of the Georgia Legislature. However, two weeks after becoming settled in Muscle Shoals, they were forced out by the Indians.

Colonel James Robertson attempted to make a settlement in Muscle Shoals in 1787, but was again forced out. A third try was made by pioneer Zachariah Cox with an armed colony and managed to stay for two years before the Indians burned the block house and small village to the ground. Cox tried to settle in Muscle Shoals one more time but was again driven out.

A Russian Princess In Early Alabama

A story often repeated in historical accounts of the early days of the future state of Alabama includes the tale of a Russian princess arriving on the shores of Alabama. She may have been a Russian princess or she may not. Some people said that she was only a wardrobe maid who had learned to imitate her mistress. Her story will forever remain a mystery, but it includes the beautiful love story that follows.

Alexei Petrovich, son of Peter the Great of Russia, married a beautiful and accomplished young woman whose name was Charlotte. But Alexis Petrowitz was a very mean, low sort of a prince who treated his lovely wife brutally. To escape from her cruel husband, the young princess pretended to die and she was buried in a tomb. Her friends came a few hours later and took her away.

Alexei Petrovich, son of Peter the Great

They put her aboard a German ship with two hundred German immigrants, all of whom came to find peace and comfort in the new world.

Chevalier D'Aubant was a French officer in the Duke of Brunswick's court who had arrived with colonial troops in 1718 and with the consent of the local Native Americans, he built a retreat on the bayou of the Gulf of Mexico.

In 1721, a young woman dressed in inexpensive garments and using the name Elizabeth arrived. She asked to be taken to D'Aubant who immediately recognized her. He declared that he had seen the young woman in St. Petersburg and knew perfectly well that she really was the daughter-in-law of Peter the Great.

The following facts provide some validity to this story.

- Alexei Petrovich was the son Peter the Great
- Petrovich married Charlotte of Brunswick-Wolfenbüttel against his will.
- Petrovich was unhappy with Charlotte. He insisted on separate apartments and ignored her in public
- They had two children, Natalia and Peter.
- Petrovich brought his long-time Finnish mistress to live in the palace after the birth of Natalia.
- Charlotte died on October 11, 1715 after giving birth to son Peter.

Elizabeth (Charlotte) and D'Aubant were supposedly married the day after she arrived. It is said that they planted two oaks on the St. John River on the wedding day which may still be standing. They lived in Mobile for some time where D 'Aubant had his headquarters.

One day the French officer told his wife that he had been ordered to take charge of Fort Toulouse near the present town of Wetumpka. He kissed his wife and little daughter goodbye, promised that they should soon join him and then set out on horseback for his new post. The one-time princess waited from March until June, then she determined to join her husband.

With one servant and her little daughter, D'Aubant's wife set out from Mobile in a rude little boat and traveled for days and days up the river toward Fort Toulouse.

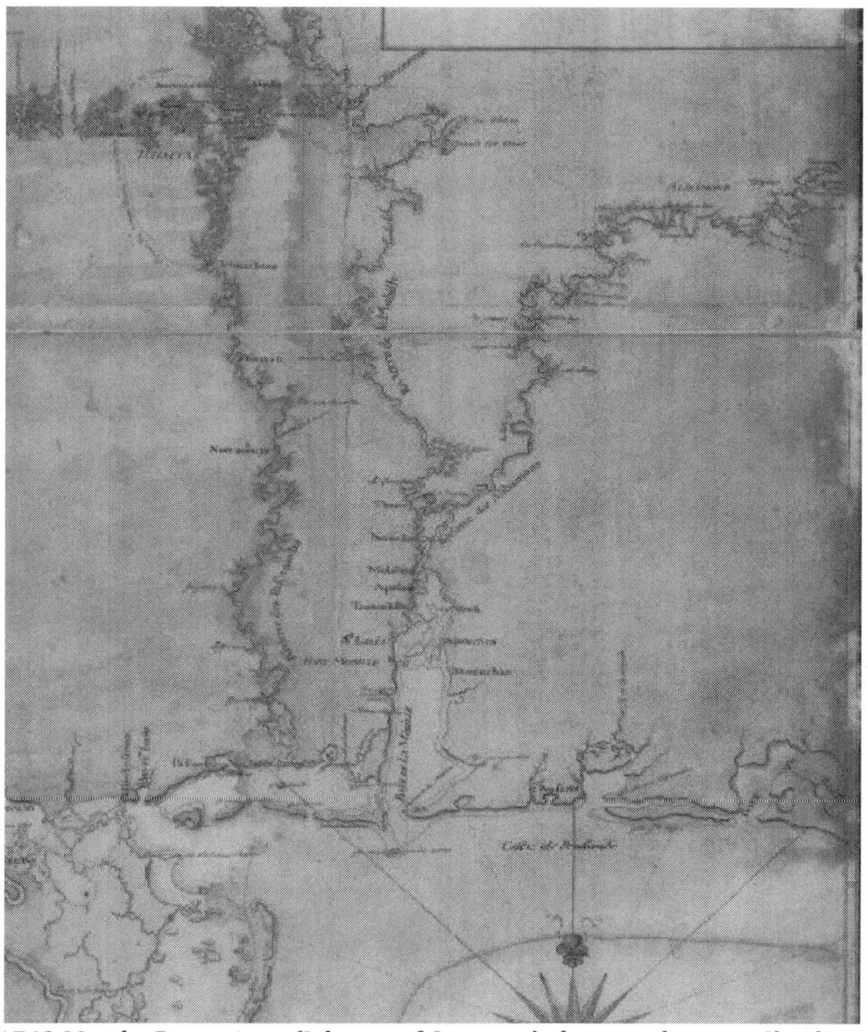

1743 Map by Demarigny (Library of Congress) showing distance Charlotte and maid traveled from Mobile by river (bottom center) up the rivers to Fort Toulouse (Upper right corner)

She finally arrived at the fort and received a royal welcome. D'Aubant was overjoyed to see his family again and the men of the fort began at once building a cabin for the D'Aubants.

The brick chimney of this cabin stood for years on the outskirts of the old town of Wetumpka and the residents always pointed out to visitors the place where a Russian princess once made her home. When at last D'Aubant returned to France, his wife and daughter followed him, but the beautiful princess never forgot her exciting experiences in the land they called Louisiana.

Alliances Create Division Among Native Americans

Three countries, England, Spain & France, claimed parts of the newly explored land in American which included the future state of Alabama. Since the majority of land in Alabama was still occupied mainly by Native Americans, the three countries encouraged the Native Americans to join forces with them and drive the rival countries out. The alliances formed created division within the Native American population residing within the future state of Alabama.

The English Carolinas were desirous of interposing a barrier between themselves and the Spaniards of the Floridas on the one hand and the French of Louisiana on the other. To carry out this desire, James Oglethorpe proposed to establish a colony upon the western bank of the Savannah in Georgia.

In February, 1733, Oglethorpe landed on that river with thirty families, numbering one hundred and twenty-five persons, and immediately laid out the city of Savannah. Calling the chiefs of the Lower Creek Nation together, he obtained from them a cession of all the lands between the Savannah and the Altamaha.

During the following year this colony was increased by a company of forty Jews; of three hundred and forty-one Germans, and by many Scots, who settled at Darien. Two years later the town of Augusta, Georgia was laid out, and a fort established there. Augusta became the scene of an active trade with the Indians. Over six hundred whites were engaged in this trade.

A highway was constructed between Augusta and Savannah, and boats plied between those towns and Charleston. After only five years from the landing of Oglethorpe, the colony of Georgia had received more than one thousand settlers from the trustees of the company, and several hundred more who came at their own expense.

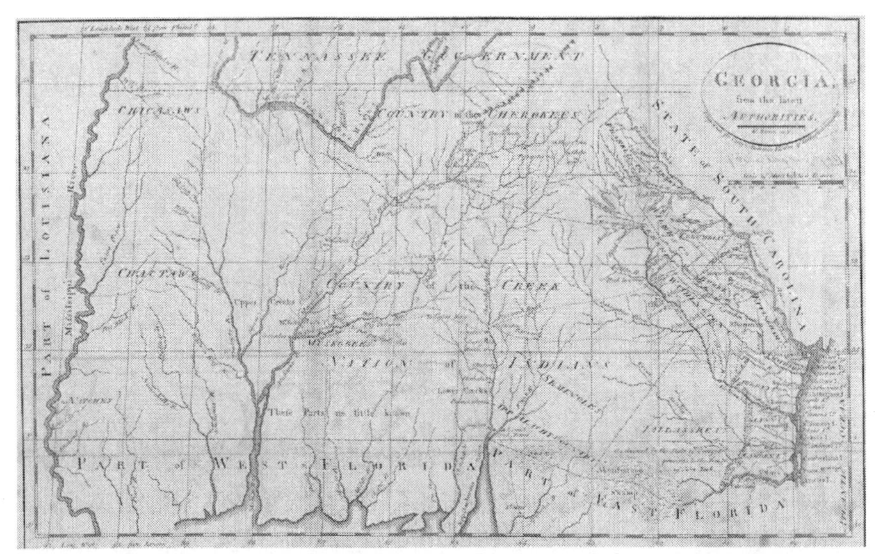

1795 map by William Barker (Library of Congress)shows Native American territory in the center and Mississippi River on far left

Georgia claimed all the territory from its eastern border to the Mississippi as belonging to her under the charter granted to Oglethorpe. As the colony filled with population, the tendency was to continually press westward. The Native Americans opposed it as trespassing upon them west of the Ocmulgee. The result was frequent clashings between the English settlers and the Native Americans. When war broke out between England and France, the Native Americans usually allied with the French.

The rapid growth of Georgia alarmed the Spanish Government and led to a series of skirmishes between the English and Floridian Spaniards. Oglethorpe wisely formed alliance with the Lower Creeks. In their treaty it was stipulated that no one but the trustees of the colony of Georgia should settle the lands between the Savannah and the mountains.

The Upper Creeks being under French and Spanish influence did not unite in this treaty. They never recognized the cessions to Oglethorpe made by the Lower Creeks. Although the English held a garrison at Octuskee on the eastern bank of the Tallapoosa river within forty miles of Fort Toulouse which had been established by Bienville, they only succeeded in converting to their cause a few of the Upper Creeks.

By May, 1736, Bienville was determined to destroy the last vestige of the Natchez tribe, who had fled from French arms upon the Mississippi, and who were now hospitably entertained by the Chickasaws in the hills of North Mississippi and North Alabama.

These Natchez refugees bore a deadly hatred for the French due to the destruction of their tribe, and lost no occasion to instill animosity against their conquerors in the breasts of the brave mountaineers. The English fanned the flame until the French were goaded by constant attacks upon their settlements to launch an expedition against the Natchez village which had been established in the heart of the Chickasaw nation.

It was planned that D'Artaquette should lead a force of French with their allies of the tribes of the Miamis and the Illinois from a point upon the Mississippi, and they should march eastward toward the heart of the Chickasaw tribe. At the same time, Bienville was to move up the Tombigbee from Mobile and march westward to the same point. The two forces would unite and extinguish the Natchez survivors and destroy English influence with the mountain tribes.

D'Artaquette reached the point of contemplated junction of forces, but could hear nothing of Bienville. He determined to make the attack alone and reap all the glory. His force consisted of one hundred and thirty Frenchmen and three hundred and sixty Indians. He charged the Natchez town and found himself confronted by a body of thirty Englishmen and five hundred Chickasaws.

The Miamis and Illinois fled at once and the French were shot down by scores. Most of the officers were slain, and D'Artaquette himself fell into the hands of the enemy and was subsequently burned to death. However, a small remnant of the expedition escaped. The French guns and ammunition captured on the field were afterwards turned against Bienville.

With an army of five hundred and fifty French and six hundred Choctaw allies, Bienville embarked at Mobile and ascended the Tombigbee to the head of navigation, now known as Cotton-Gin Port. Not hearing from

D'Artaquette, he marched westward twenty-seven miles and encountered the first Chickasaw village.

To his astonishment he found it well fortified by stockades with loop-holes for musketry, and with the English flag flying over the fort. Bienville attacked the village and was most disgracefully driven back. His Choctaw allies gave him no assistance in the battle. He left his dead and wounded on the field of Pontotoc and hastily reached the river and descended to Mobile. This disastrous expedition terminated the official career of Bienville.

Traders

Traders From Scotland Marry Native Americans

There are perhaps few regions of the world, outside of the motherland of Scotland, where there can be found a larger proportion of population bearing the family names of the great Highland clans than in Alabama—especially in the southern and eastern parts of the State.

In almost every county or even a neighborhood in Alabama one can find either Camerons, Campbells, Fergusons, Frasers, Gordons, Grahams, McDonalds, McKenzies, Mclntoshes, McLeans, McLeods, McNeills, McPhersons, McMillans, Stewarts or others with distinctly Highland names.

Hard economic conditions, as well as political and religious disturbances, sent the Scots of every breed among the pioneers into many of the newer lands of the world. When they arrived in a new home, they did not segregate themselves from other peoples, but instead mingled and frequently married with their earlier inhabitants.

Two Scots, Lachlan McGillivray and Charles Weatherford, who were traders and adventurers, settled in the Creek Indian territory. They established themselves in the region of the junction of the Coosa and Tallapoosa rivers near the Native American town which was located in the flat, southern part of Wetumpka.

Lachlan McGillivray married a Native American girl, Sehoy, in 1745. She was the daughter of Marchand by an Native American woman of the tribe of the Wind. Marchand had been commander of Fort Toulouse. After his marriage to her, he did business both here and at Little Tallasse, and accumulated quite a fortune.

Hickory Ground is also known as Otciapofa, and is an historic Upper Muscogee Creek tribal town, now located in Elmore County, Alabama and was home to several thousand Muscogee. In the Muscogee language, it is known as Oce Vpofa. It is best known for serving as the last capital of the

National Council of the Creek Nation, prior to the tribe being moved to the Indian Territory in the 1830s. During the Creek War, the inhabitants who were not fighting in the war were confined at nearby Fort Jackson.

After the end of the war, they were allowed to resettle the site and remained there until 1832, when they forced them to move to the Indian Territory in Oklahoma. The town was added to the National Register of Historic Places on March 10, 1980. It is a former village with a ceremonial ground, burial grounds, and refuse sites. The site was documented during historic times by Naturalist, William Bartram in the 1760s and Indian Agent, Benjamin Hawkins, in 1799.

Drawing of Alexander McGillivray

The son of Lachlan by the Native American princess, Alexander McGillivray, became a powerful man among the Creeks. He was carefully educated at Charleston, and at the age of 30 was elected Chief of the Creek Nation around the time of the outbreak of the American Revolutionary War.

The British commissioned him a colonel, and thus early secured his favor. He was active in confederating the Native Americans against the Whigs, and led many expeditions of Tory Refugees and Native Americans against the white settlements of the Gulf.

Charles Weatherford was a Scots trader known for his red hair. He married Sehoy III, a high-status Creek woman of the Wind Clan. She was of French and possibly of Scottish descent. Charles Weatherford estabished a trading post near the Creek village upon the first eastern bluff below the confluence of the Coosa and Tallapoosa, and laid out the first race-paths ever known in East Alabama. There he developed a large plantation as well as raised thoroughbred race horses.

He and Sehoy III were the parents of Creek Chief Red Eagle William Weatherford who was born near the Upper Creek town of Coosauda (now Coosada) and Hickory Ground (now Wetumpka). Chief Red Eagle led the Upper Creek towns, the Red Sticks, in the Creek War against the United States which occurred in 1813-14.

Another prominent immigrant from Scotland was Captain McIntosh, a Loyalist during the American Revolutionary War. He had worked with the Creek Native Americans to recruit them as military allies to the British.

His mother was believed to be Jennet/Janet McGillivray, a sister of Lacklan McGillivray. Captain McIntosh was the father of Chief White Warrior William McIntosh. Chief McIntosh's mother was a member of the Wind Clan of the Creeks.

Chief William McIntosh

After the Revolutionary War, Captain McIntosh moved from the frontier to Savannah, Georgia to settle. He married a paternal cousin, Barbara McIntosh and established a plantation there.

Chief McIntosh, his son. was considered a skilled orator and politician; he became a wealthy planter and slaveholder; and he was influential in both Creek and European-American society.

For generations, Creek chiefs encouraged and approved their daughters' marriages to fur traders to strengthen their alliances and trading power with wealthy Europeans.

All over the territory of Alabama and Mississippi, wherever an Indian town of importance was found, white traders lived. Some of them became wealthy.

Native American Government Trading Houses Established

By the Act of Congress, on April 18, 1796, the establishment of government trading houses was authorized. Native American trading houses were established shortly after the Revolutionary War to create a more satisfied and friendly feeling among the Native Americans toward the government. The first trading house in Alabama was at Fort St. Stephens.

Soon there were established fourteen trading posts among various tribes. They were established as follows:

1. Coleraine on the St. Mary's River, Georgia, 1795
2. Tellico block house, or Hiwasee, Tennessee, 1795
3. Fort St. Stephen, Alabama, 1802
4. Chickasaw Bluffs, later Memphis, Tenn., 1802
5. Fort Wayne, Indiana, 1802
6. Detroit, Michigan, 1802
7. Arkansas, on the river Arkansas, 1805
8. Natchitoches on Red River, Louisiana, 1805
9. Belle Fontaine, at mouth of the Missouri River, 1805
10. Chicago, Lake Michigan, 1805
11. Sandusky. Lake Erie. 1806
12. On the Island of Michilimackinac, Lake Huron. Michigan, 1808
13. Fort Osage, on the Missouri River, Missouri, 1808
14. Fort Madison, 1808

Detroit was discontinued in 1805, and Belle Fontaine in 1808. The post at Coleraine, Georgia, was moved to Fort Wilkinson in 1797 and again to Fort Hawkins in 1806.

The United States hoped by the establishment of these trading houses to create a more satisfied and friendly feeling among the Native Americans toward the government. It was designed to bring to them in their own territory, such supplies as would add to their domestic comfort and at a price that would undersell the private trader. For a time the policy seemed to be most successful, but gradually the Government came more and more to see that the system was a failure.

Every trading house was protected by U. S. soldiers and the factors, in most cases, thus protected, were indifferent as to whether the Native Americans were in a friendly attitude toward him or not, while the private trader, being constantly in their power, became identified with the tribe which he commonly visited.

Again, the Government factors, generally, carelessly allowed their stock to become inferior, and of such character as was not suited to the needs of the Native Americans, while the private trader carried just what they wanted.

The Choctaw Trading house in Alabama was established at Fort St. Stephen in 1802. The first factor was Joseph Chambers, who was instrumental in bringing into Alabama from Tennessee, George S. Gaines, who served as his assistant until 1807, when he succeeded Chambers as factor.

The building occupied by the factor being old and inadequate, a new brick warehouse was built near the old Fort. This was probably the first brick house within the bounds of the present State of Alabama. This trading house under the management of Mr. Gaines was highly satisfactory. He fully realized the importance of his position and the mission he had to perform and was proud of the results of his labors.

The business of the trading house increased wonderfully. Not only did the Choctaws frequent the post, but also the Creeks, from the Black Warrior River, and even the Chickasaws. Mr. Gaines was careful to treat all fairly and justly. If the goods was defective or inferior, he pointed it out to the Native Americans and reduced the price. Consequently he won their utmost respect and confidence.

The settlement of St. Stephens is now-abandoned, but once a steady stream of immigrants came into the State of Alabama and as the white population about St. Stephens grew and multiplied, it was found advisable to move the trading house farther into the Choctaw country.

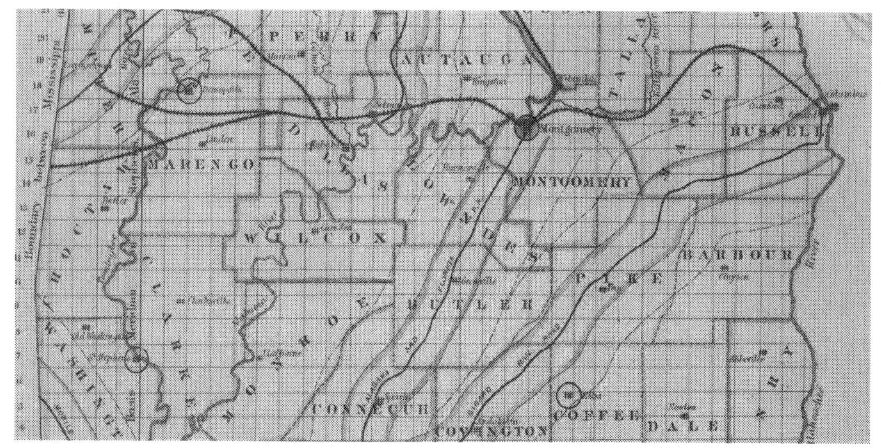

1866 Alabama map showing St. Stephens

on lower left side with circle.

St. Stephens was located atop a limestone bluff overlooking the Tombigbee River 67 miles north of Mobile in present-day Washington County. The settlement later hosted Alabama's first seat of government. Today the site of the town is referred to as Old St. Stephens and is a historical park and archeological site.

George S. Gaines called on the famous Choctaw Chief, Pushmataha to advise a suitable location. He suggested the site of the old Fort Tombecbe, the Spanish Fort Confederation. Work upon the new post immediately began and on its completion in May, 1816, the post was opened to active trade with the Native Americans.

In October of the same year, the U. S. War Department authorized Colonel McKee to arrange for a treaty to be held at the Choctaw trading house in order that new sessions of lands might be secured from the Native Americans. The chiefs and commissioners spent several days discussing all sides of the question till October 24th, when the treaty was signed. By this treaty all of Alabama, with the exception of the territory of the Cherokees in the lower Tennessee Valley, was open to white settlement.

John Hersey succeeded Gaines as factor in October, 1819, and served so long as the trading house existed.

The entire system of Government trading houses was abolished by act of Congress, May 6, 1822.

Traders Used Pack-horses To Transport Their Merchandise

The Wheat and Mounger families lived near St. Stephens and are considered by many historians to have been the first Whig families that settled among the Royalists. It is probable, however, that there were at the time other settlers loyal to the United States may have lived further away.

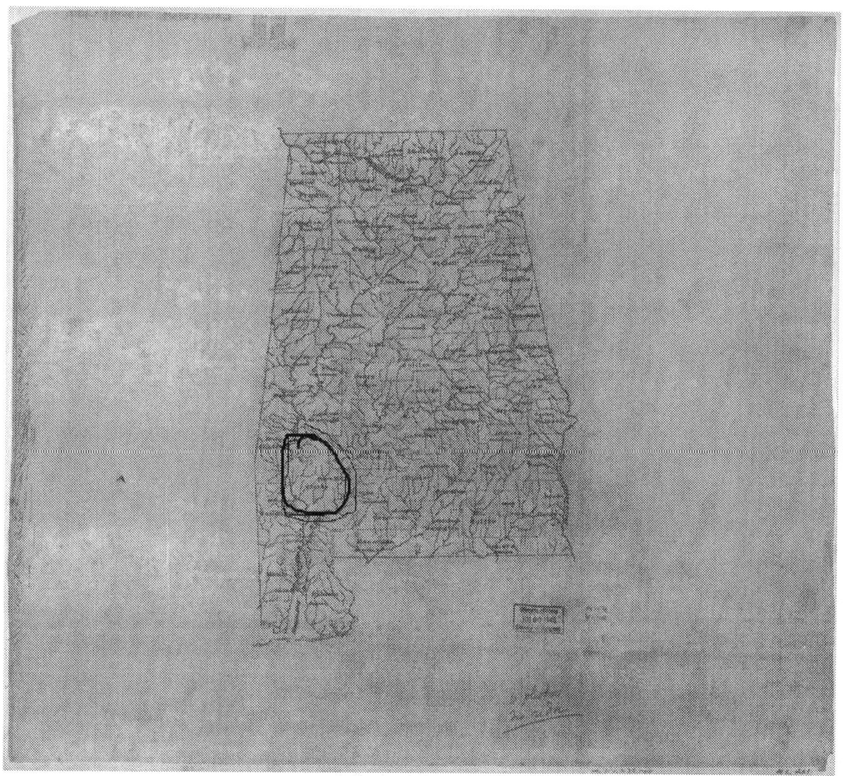

1893 Map of Alabama showing Clarke County, Alabama with a circle.

Hiram Mounger came in 1791, bought a Spanish grant, including a part of the Sun Flower Bend. One of the three grants is now known as having been situated on the east side of the river. He died about 1867, and his wife died a few years later between ninety and one hundred years of age.

In 1790, Nathan Blackwell is said to have come from North Carolina to Clarke county, Alabama He was a pioneer among Indians and Spaniards. Other family names in Clarke county include Denby, a brother-in-law of Mounger, and Peter Beach.

"All these settlements were around the area of old Maubila. But few if any of the pioneers destined to occupy those creek bottoms, and broad plateaus, and fertile hill sides, had as yet arrived. This soil was never occupied by an American colony, it was not yet an acknowledged part of the United States, although its southern limit was thirteen miles north of latitude 31°; and those who were to take possession as American citizens were then, for the most part, boys and girls in Virginia and Kentucky, in the Carolinas and Georgia, acquiring the strength of muscle, and the qualities of mind and heart which would fit them for their future work."

At the time of their arrival, laws were few, restraints were only self-imposed, or such as necessity and self-preservation laid upon them, and they, no doubt, enjoyed the wild freedom of the rivers and the woods. A characteristic feature of this region was the residence in every Indian town of any size of a white trader. The sight of white women and children was more rare.

Traders had penetrated all the wilds, and occupied very many fine locations for inland commerce and for intrigues among the tribes. Many of these traders became wealthy. One of these traders, an Englishman named Clarke, who called his Indian wife Queen Anne, used seventy pack-horses to transport his goods and furs.

The common pack-horses used were small but hardy, and were accustomed to carry on their peculiar pack-saddles, three bundles of sixty pounds weight each. Two bundles were swung across the saddle so that one was on each side of the horse, and the third bundle was placed upon the saddle. Over the whole was thrown a covering of hide or fur to protect from the rain. Poultry was carried in a similar manner, and also liquids, on the backs or sides of these ponies.

On the routes of travel one pack-driver had charge of ten ponies. About twenty-five miles each day was the average rate of travel. The ponies at night gained their own subsistence from the grass and cane. A well-beaten trail led up from Pensacola, with many smaller diverging pathways to the Tennessee river.

Nashville, on the Cumberland, was then the southern limit of white settlement. But from the Wabash river, far north, Vincennes having become a trading-post as early as 1702, French traders had for years, previous to 1780, carried on an extensive traffic with the Indians near the present towns of Tuscumbia and Florence. Southern and Western forests during the eighteenth century were anything but pathless.

The presence of these white traders throughout all Indian country had a strong influence on the Indians as well as white residents almost immediately after a settlement was made.

A Ruse Saved Immigrants Lives While Traveling Through Native American Territory

When war finally broke out between England and France in 1752 the Chickasaws remained true to the English, and Bienville's successor, the Marquis De Vaudreuil, determined to chastise them. He pursued the route followed by Bienville landed with his army at Cotton Gin Port, marched westward against the Chickasaw villages, but he was beaten as disastrously as his predecessor had been. He returned to Mobile with no laurels.

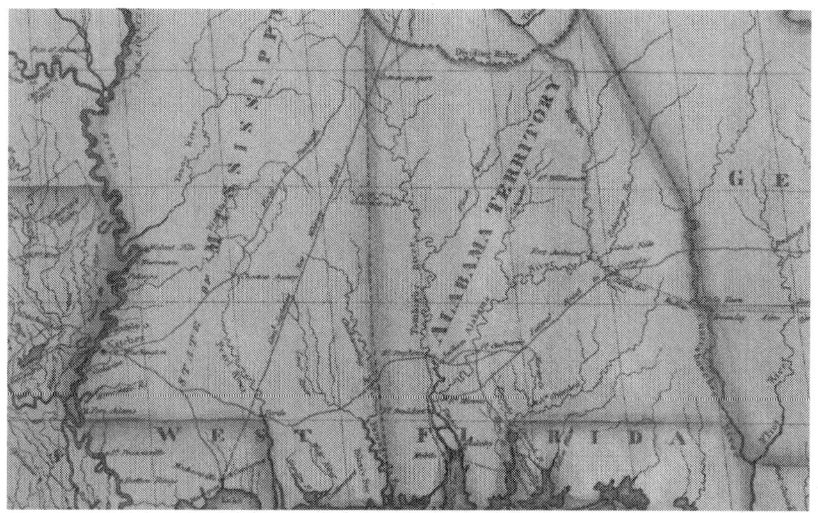

1819 Map by John L. Narstin shows Tombigbee River to the left boundary of Alabama Territory with Cotton Gin Port at top and Mobile at bottom. (Library of Congress)

At the conclusion of the French and Indian war, by treaty of February 18, 1763, France ceded to Great Britain all of her Canadian possessions and all of Louisiana lying on the eastern side of the Mississippi, as far south as Bayou Iberville. She ceded also the port and river of Mobile.

Spain, the ally of France, ceded to Great Britain her province of Florida. The northern boundary of West Florida was declared to be the line 32 degrees, 28 minutes, which, commencing at the mouth of the Yazoo river, extended through points near the towns of Demopolis on the Tombigbee, and of Columbus on the Chattahoochee. Alabama, south of that line, was in British West Florida; and Alabama, north of that line, was in British Illinois.

As soon as the fertile lands of Alabama and Mississippi passed into English hands, and a British Governor was stationed at Mobile, Anglo-American colonies sprang up in every direction.

A colony of North Carolinians settled between Manchac and Baton Rouge. Virginians came down the Ohio and the Tennessee. Many immigrants came in from England, Ireland, Scotland and the British West Indies.

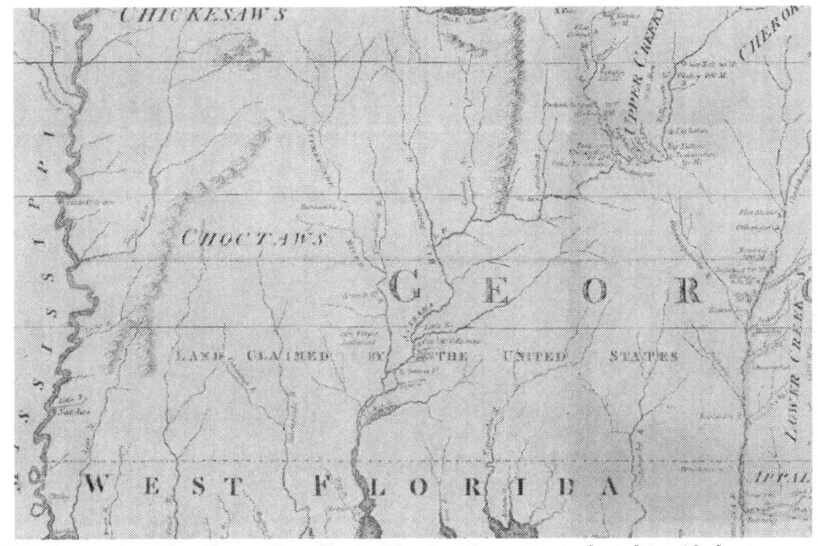

1796 map by Abraham Bradley - Native American land in Alabama and some trading houses to Northeast (Library of Congress)

All along the Mississippi and covering a belt of fifteen miles; settled adventurers from New Jersey, Delaware, and Virginia, and colonies of Scots and of Germans, many of whom assumed French names. The British government industriously supplied early settlers with African slaves.

Trips across the wilds of early Alabama were not without peril. In 1781, a party of Americans from about Natchez, Mississippi, numbering about one hundred men, women, and children, led by Colonel Hutchins, came to the Native American town of Hickory Ground. They sympathized with the British, and were in danger about Natchez because the opposers of British rule had obtained the ascendency there. The party was trying to make their way to Savannah, Georgia and had wandered at times much out of the way.

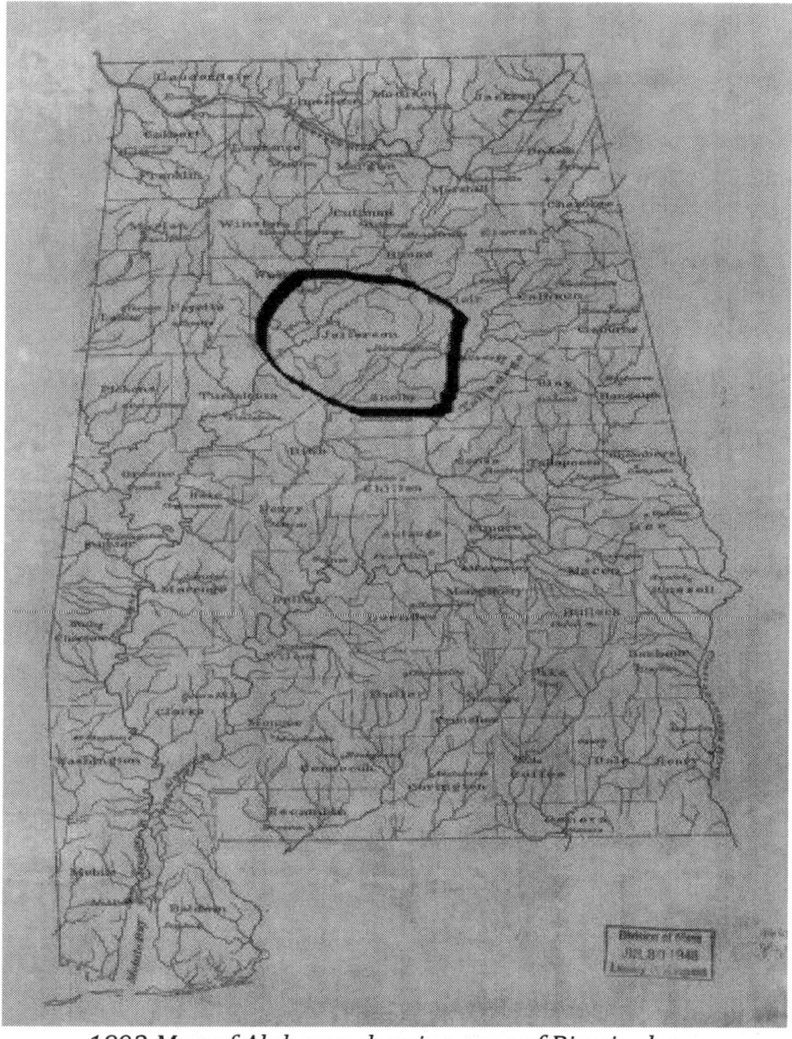

1893 Map of Alabama showing area of Birmingham

When they reached the vicinity of where Birmingham, Alabama now stands, they became afraid to venture among the Cherokee Indians, and turning from the mountains southeasterly, made their way toward the Native American town of Hickory Ground where Wetumpka now stands.

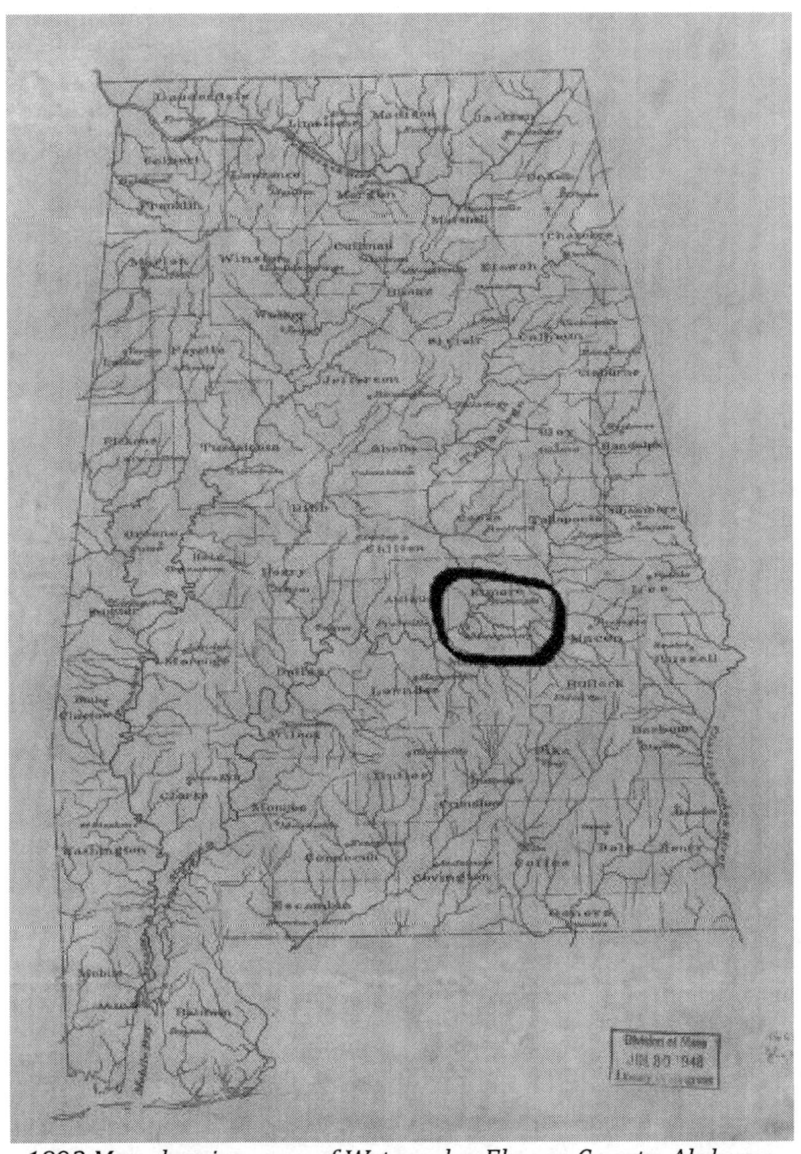

1893 Map showing area of Wetumpka, Elmore County, Alabama

One of the party was a Mrs. Dwight, who on at least two occasions during their trip, had proved herself quite a heroine. They came to the Coosa River about twenty miles above Hickory Ground and hesitated about what to do.

Mrs. Dwight urged upon them to cross the river and pursue their way, and leading herself, they crossed partly by fording and partly by swimming. When they came to the town, the Trading Post Agent, McGillivray, was away. The Indians took them for a party of Georgians who they hated, and threatened to destroy them. The party begged earnestly for mercy, and disclaimed being Georgians. They told the Indians their story of escape from, Natchez, and their efforts to reach the English at Savannah.

The Indians, intent on their destruction, would have accomplished it but for a ruse practiced by a smart African-American body servant of McGillivray, named Paro, who was present. The Indians told the party they would not believe their story unless they "could make the paper talk," that is, by a written statement.

Since Paro could speak English, he listened to their story. Getting some paper from one of the Hutchins party, he pretended to read from it the story of their flight, how they had suffered, and were then badly bruised up and worn out, and were only trying to reach their own people.

When the Indians heard the paper talk corroborating what had been said, they gladly received them, fed them, and cared for them until, rested and refreshed. And they they were permitted again to go on their way.

Postal Routes

Isaac Briggs Risks His Life To Map A Road

Once the United States acquired New Orleans and the Louisiana Territory through the Lousiana purchase from France in 1803, President Jefferson and other leaders recognized the need for a survey of the Territory and better communication with the settled area along the Mississippi River. Jefferson's administration developed plans for roads to be cut throughout the Mississippi Territory and the Indian nations.

Benjamin Hawkins served in the Continental Army on George Washington's staff as his main interpreter of French. He was appointed General Superintendent for Indian Affairs by President George Washington in 1796.

Mississippi Territory 1798

In 1804, at the request of United States Secretary of War Dearborn, Benjamin Hawkins was instructed to talk to the Creeks about establishing road through the Creek Nation.

While the talks were proceeding, President Thomas Jefferson asked the Surveyor General of the Mississippi Territory, Isaac Briggs, to travel from Washington, DC back to Natchez in the Mississippi Territory "via the Indian paths Hawkins had traveled a few years earlier." The purpose of this trip was to provide President Jefferson with a true length of a potential mail route based on scientific measurements.

Briggs journey across the Creek Nation nearly killed him. He and "his assistant Thomas Robertson entered the Creek Nation from Georgia on October 6, 1804 without a guide and immediately became lost. They wandered many miles astray in the wilderness" until they came upon the store of an Native American trader. Then severe storms delayed them.

They failed to procure a guide to Hawkins post sixty miles away, but decided to set out again. For a second time they became lost. Briggs stated that they probably wandered at least 112 miles, "frequently climbing over precipices, wading through swamps, and crossing deep and difficult water courses, many miles without a path, our horses greatly incommoded and fatigued by sensitive briers and other vines. Our provisions were soon wet and spoiled and we were in danger of starving, not having seen a human face except each other's for more than four days. On the 15th we arrived at Colonel Hawkins's on Flint River."

They stayed with Hawkins five days to recover and Benjamin Hawkins restocked them with supplies and a guide for their continued trip to Point Comfort which was located south of Tuckaubatchee. Again a heavy rain caused the rivers and streams to be swollen and their horses had to swim the Chattahoochee River from shore to shore.

They left Point Comfort and finally arrived at the "house of Nathaniel Christmas, on the west side of the Tombigbee River," in early November. Word of a yellow fever outbreak in New Orleans caused the pair to delay the last leg of their trip.

Briggs' difficulties and the calculations he and his partner Robertson made provided some value by mapping a mail route across the Creek Nation that would save about 500 miles compared to the previous

Applachian/Natchez Trace route.

Benjamin Hawkins Established A Mail Route

Benjamin Hawkins grew up among the planter elite in North Carolina and was a delegate to the Continental Congress. He learned the Muscogee language and married Lavinia Downs who some believe was a Creek woman. They had seven children and lived in Crawford, Georgia.

President George Washington appointed him the principal Indian agent to the Creek Native Americans. Hawkins as well as other American leaders negotiated treaties with the Indian nations to establish *horse paths* across the Native American land to be used by U. S. post riders, military troops, and other Americans.

In these treaties, they offered the Native American chiefs who signed for their people the opportunity to operate causeways, ferries and houses of entertainment along the horse paths which allowed the "chiefs to benefit from tolls, lodging fares and tavern tabs."

The main purpose of the horse trails was to establish a route for efficient mail service. "In August 1806, Postmaster General Gideon Granger contracted with Joseph Wheaton to establish a postal route between Athens, Georgia, and Fort Stoddert, Mississippi Territory, generally coinciding with the path followed for years by travelers through the Creek Nation."

Wheaton found his task more difficult than he imagined. He and his men became so seriously ill with fever that they abandoned the clearing project after only two weeks and he attempted to contract out the contract. Even this failed.

Finally, a mail route was established through the Creek Nation by Benjamin Hawkins who worked with the U. S. military to make the route passable for horses and hired Creek Indians as post riders.

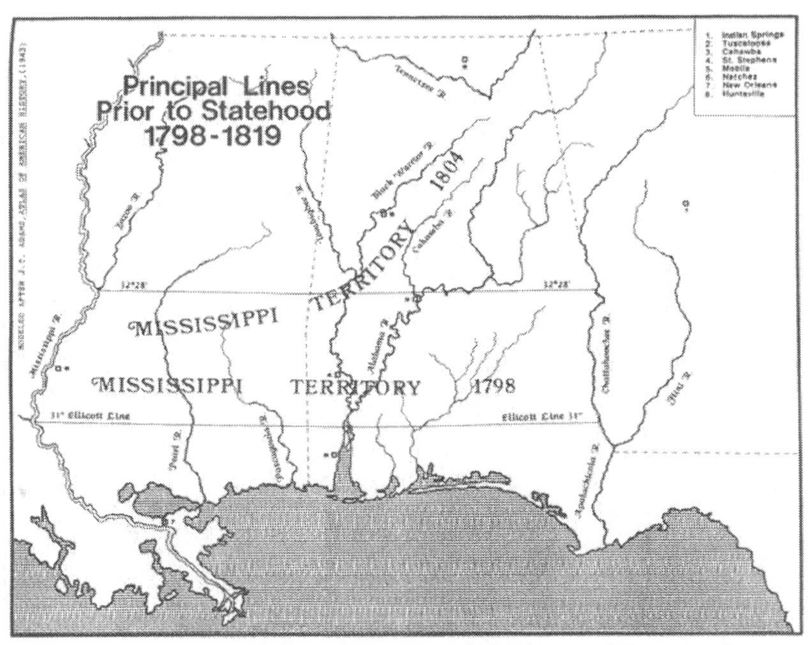

Lines prior to Alabama Statehood (Library of Congress)

Hawkins also encouraged the Creek Indians to establish *houses of entertainment* along the route. Several Creeks such as William McIntosh, Samuel Moniac, and James Cornells took advantage of this opportunity.

These *houses of entertainment* eventually became stagecoach stops, inns, taverns as well as relay points for postal riders. They were situated about 16 miles apart which was considered an average day's travel for foot traffic.

Travel To Alabama

Before The Federal Road

French trade from Mobile was principally by the river, but there was a land route to Fort Toulouse, which doubtless joined the one from Pensacola, running through thick forests south of the Alabama to the same place.

The traders generally went in companies of fifteen to twenty men, with perhaps seventy to eighty pack and other horses. The horses were permitted to graze at night and the start in the morning was after the sun was high. The loaded animals fell into single file, and were urged on with whip and whoop at a lively pace.

Lorenzo Dow

An instance of the difference between traveling before and after the Federal Road was cut may be found in the life of the eccentric but earnest

Methodist preacher Lorenzo Dow.

In 1803 he was in Georgia and set out for Tombigbee, by way of the agency of Hawkins, who "treated them cool." In thirteen and a half days after leaving the Georgia settlements they reached the first house in the Tensaw district.

His only notice of the "road or rather Indian path" was that they lost it once and then it took a good woodsman to find it again. He preached at Tensaw on a Sunday, and kept also a string of appointments across the swamp and the rivers. This was at a thick settlement, which must have been about McIntosh Bluff, and a scattered one above, seventy miles long. It then took him six and a half days to reach the Natchez settlement.

1823 Map of south Georgia, Alabama, Louisiana, & West Florida (Library of Congress)

At the end of December, 1804, he returned, but the only road he mentioned is the trading road from the Chickasaws to Mobile, near Dinsmore's agency and Fort St. Stephen. At St. Stephens he found but one family. He seems to have tarried six days in the Tensaw settlement, holding meetings, and in early January traveled on to Georgia.

Old Tavern in Talladega County, Alabama

(W. N. Manning photographer - Library of Congress)

In the Creek nation there were so many by-paths as to make it difficult to find their way. Charges for entertainment were high. On the first trip near Tensaw he paid $1.50 for a night's lodging, and now at Hawkins' eleven shillings, "although not worth the half."

Later his wife, Peggy Dow, recounts a similar trip east by way of the Bigbee settlement in December, but does not give the year. It was Lorenzo's tenth passage, however, to and from Natchez.

There seems to have been an Indian path, crossing a slough called a "Hell Hole," and they went over a river by night. They "staid two or three days in the St. Stephens neighborhood," and she notes "the Tombigbee there as beautiful, with water clear as crystal. St. Stephens was small but made a handsome appearance." They crossed by a ferry and in a day and a half passed over the Alabama too, a beautiful river, "almost beyond description." This was probably at or near what is now Claiborne.

They then struck the road cut by order of the president from Georgia to

Fort Stoddard (sic.) They frequently met people on it removing to the Tombigbee and other parts of Mississippi Territory. The road having been newly cutout, the fresh marked trees served for a guide; there was a moon but it was shut by clouds.

The troubles of immigrants on these routes can well be pictured from the journal of Rev. John Owen, describing the removal of his family in 1818 by wagon from near Norfolk, Virginia, to Tuscaloosa, Alabama. The roads in old settled Virginia he declares bad enough, but, after he passed through Beauford's Gap of the Alleghanies and descended the Holston Valley via Knoxville, sickness, upsets, breakages and discouragements were their daily experience. Even before he reached East Tennessee he wished that he had not been born.

Between "infernal roads" and straying horses, he declared "the Devil turned loose" in good earnest. He seems to have gone down the Sequatchee Valley to the Tennessee River. Exactly where he crossed into Alabama Territory in the Cherokee boundaries does not appear, and the only definite point named in the eight days between there and his destination is Jones' Valley, near modern Birmingham. Possibly he crossed at Nickajack and from the Georgia road went down Wills' Valley, along the route of the present Alabama Great Southern Railroad.

In Alabama he found the smiths lazy, meal scarce, corn and fodder high, and people rough and "shuffling," but he does make one of his few entries of "roads good," and he does not mention as many accidents at this end of his route as before crossing our line. Maybe he had become used to them. The day after Christmas he makes the entry, "past brokenroads and got to Tuscaloosa and feel thankful to kind Heaven that after nine weeks' traveling and exposed to every danger that we arrived safe and in good health."

Women Steered The Boats While The Men Fought

There were many routes that early pioneers used to move to the newly created state of Alabama.

One route from the North Carolina/South Carolina area of the Pee Dee River. Immigrants frequently traveled with pack-horses over two hundred miles to the Holston River in northeastern Tennessee. Then they continued on to the Catawba Trail to the Wilderness Road Fort near Kingsport, Tennessee. Some may have settled along the way where these present towns are now located:

- Cheraws, South Carolina
- Wadesboro, North Carolina,
- Lenoir, North Carolina,
- Blowing Rock, North Carolina
- Boone, North Carolina
- Hampton, Tennessee
- Johnson City, Tennessee
- Kingsport, Tennessee

When they reached the Wilderness Road Fort, a flat boat was secured. The flat boats were sturdy with one end enclosed for protection from the elements. It had to be designed to allow for the women, children, food, bedding and household items.

They had to transport a milk cow, chickens, horses, hunting dogs and farm implements. Once aboard the flat boats they followed the Holston River to the Tennessee River which they entered near Knoxville, Tennessee.

They always had to be prepared for attacks by the Native Americans so women often steered the boats while the men fought.

The present day towns and cities they passed were:

- Surgoinsville, Tennessee
- Chalk Level, Tennessee
- Cherokee Lake, Tennessee
- Buffalo Springs, Tennessee
- Mascot, Tennessee

The flatboats would continue down the Tennessee River into Alabama and pass the present day cities of

- Dayton, Tennnessee
- Chattanooga, Tennessee,
- Scottsboro, Alabama
- Guntersville, Alabama
- Decatur, Alabama
- Florence, Alabama

Another route was the Natchez Trace from Nashville, Tennessee to Natchez, Mississippi.

"The Natchez Trace was one of the trails which the Native Americans allowed the settlers to use in accordance with a treaty with the United States government. It was the most traveled of the land routes into the Natchez country."

In 1806, Congress provided for the construction of the Natchez Trace to connect Nashville, Tennessee with Natchez upon the Mississippi by crossing the Tennessee River at Muscle Shoals.

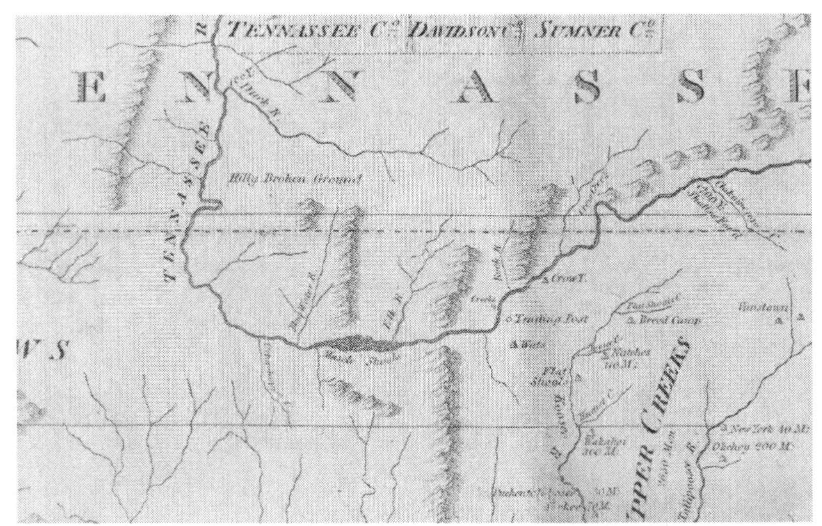

1796 map showing Tennessee River and few trading posts on bottom right by Abraham Bradley (Library of Congress)

One land route went from Knoxville to Natchez by way of the Tombigbee River. This went through the Cherokee Indian territory. The other land route to Natchez left the Oconne settlement in Georgia crossing the Alabama River to Fort Stevens and the Tombigbee River."

"The Federal Road began in 1806 as a postal road. The Creeks by that time had given permission for the development of a horse path through their nation, its purpose being a more efficient mail delivery between Washington City and New Orleans. Migration into the Mississippi Territory was slow in part due to the presence of the powerful Creek and Cherokee tribes in western Georgia and the Choctaw and Chickasaw in Alabama and Mississippi."

In 1811, when conflicts with the French had reached a point where it seemed necessary to be able to move troops and supplies quickly across the Mississippi Territory, the Federal Road was widened and improved for that purpose. This led to the Creek Indian War of 1813-14 and then to the removal of the Native Americans to the West.

The Federal Road followed the route from Athens, Georgia to New

Orleans, passing through the settlement on the Tombigbee River in Alabama.

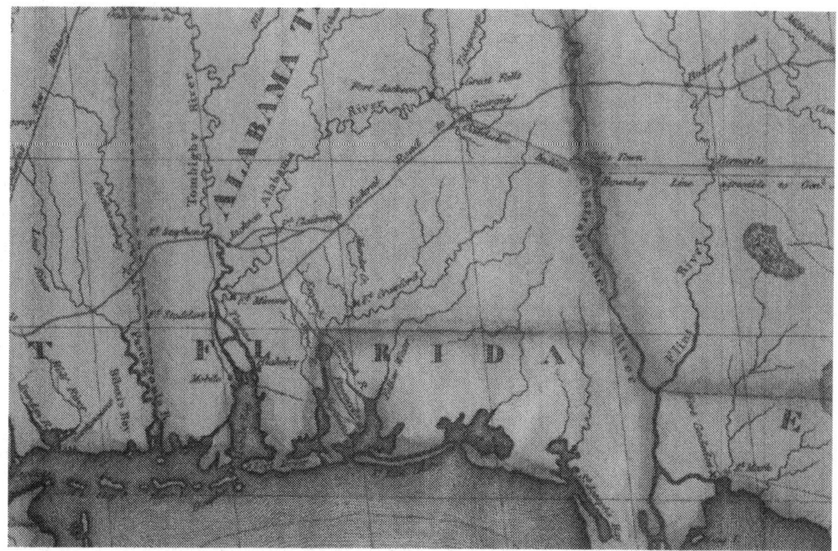

1810 Map of the Federal road from Georgia through Alabama to Mississippi

(Library of Congress)

"Many settlers made the tedious trip over the Federal Road. The major arteries of the East and North had connections that led to the newly acquired lands. Traders and light travelers from the North came down the Upper Road through the Piedmont into Georgia, then traveled over the postal horse path which had opened in 1806, through Athens, Watkinsville, and High Shoals, to meet the Federal Road at Columbus, Georgia.

Others used the somewhat easier Fall Line Road and then met the Federal Road, traveling through Augusta, Warrenton, Sparta, Milledgeville, and Macon before reaching Columbus. Crossing on through Alabama, the Federal Road ended at a crossroads known as St. Stephens" [1]

---

1 Many Maps and sketches of American migration routes can be found online at ***Early American Roads and Trails***, *Beverly Whitaker, Kansas City, Missouri, Copyright 2002*
<http://freepages.genealogy.rootsweb.com/~gentutor/trails.html>

Such were the slender bands of communication which tied the frontier settlements of the Mississippi Territory to the world from which they were separated by hundreds of miles of Native American wilderness.

Neither Indian Or White Man Was Seen

Traveling within Alabama before 1800 was treacherous. The dense vegetation and lack of roads, settlements or other structures were not available for guidance through the unknown country.

In the transcribed *Diary of Richard Brekenridge* (1781-1840), the tension in Richard Brekenridge's words are palpable as he describes his experiences while surveying the land in Marengo County, Alabama for a new homesite.

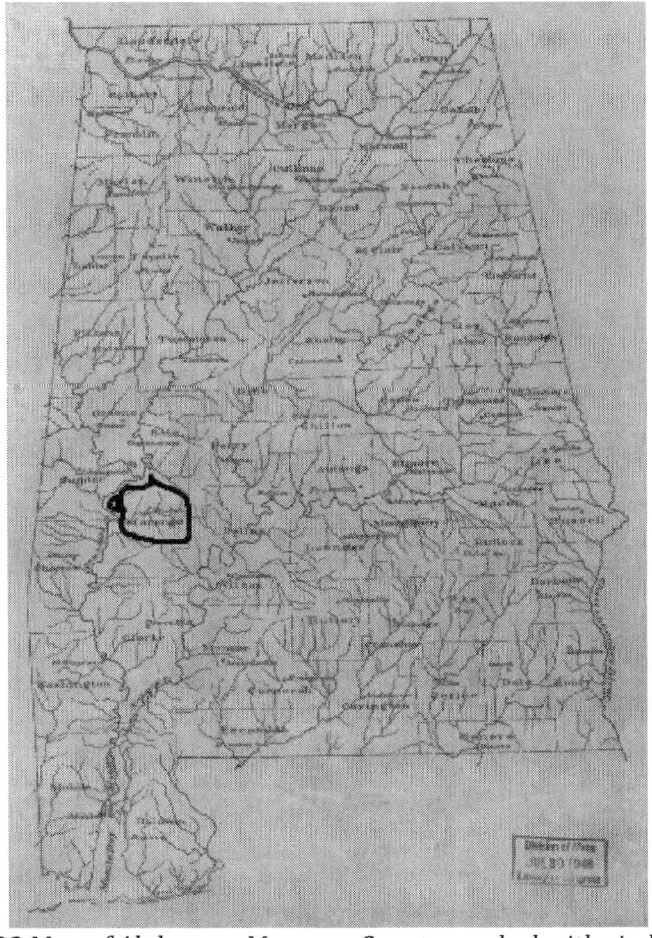

1893 Map of Alabama - Marengo County marked with circle

August 7, 1816 to my last night's camp; expect to go up the river in the morning to see if I can find inhabitants or a place to cross. I saw no good land to-day except some in the swamp. The country is very broken. I have seen neither Indians nor white men since the day I left Mr. McMilen's.[2]

August the 8th I took up the river this morning, and had a tolerable good road. About 11 o'clock, I crossed a very large creek somewhat in appearance like Big Shoal Creek and nearly as wide as Elk. There was some very good land in this creek bottom, and I suppose water might be tolerably convenient, but the country is as broken as it is on Elk. I saw this day on a creek west of this large one as beautiful a site for a mill as I ever did see—fine bluffs on both sides and a [a few words here illegible]. I have not since 12 o'clock come across one acre of tillable land, but the most broken mountainous country I ever was in. The mare is almost done, cut with bushes, briers and thorns. I intend to push in the morning to find a path to some inhabitants. I think it cannot be far from the road that leads down to the Falls from Ditto's Landing.[3]

August the 9th I started this morning a southeast course. About 12 o'clock, I came to a creek, which runs nearly my course. From its looks, its swamp appears almost impassable. I have been going down it all evening and have seen no place to cross. I am in great anxiety, having spent ten days and done nothing. This is the fifth day that I have seen neither Indian nor white man. I now repent that I did not go to Colbert at the Cotton Gin[45] and make the necessary inquiries. I had a very heavy rain today and it is yet cloudy. I had a extensive prospect to-day from the top of a very high knob, and from the appearance I have a large creek or

---

2 'It has been found impossible from available data, and in the absence of a knowledge of the local topography to follow with any particularity or certainty the route of travel from the time the diary opens on Aug. 7 to Aug. 20, when the river is reached. It appears probable that after he left his companions, he went up the Tombigbee river in the direction of Cotton Gin Port. After a day or two he abruptly changed his course to the East and South-east, in which general direction he continued until he entered Jones' Valley. All his observations show that he traveled along the South side of the water shed between the Tennessee river and the several creeks flowing into the Tombigbee and Warrior rivers. His route evidently carried him across parts of Marion, Winston and Walker Counties. Through all this region there was not a single settler.

3 Whitesburg on the Tennessee river, directly South of Huntsville was called Ditto's Landing

4 Cotton Gin Port, Miss., is on the Tombigbee river North of Aberdeen, and near the present Amory, on the Kansas City, Memphis and Birmingham R. R.

5 See map page 39 for Cotton Gin Port

river yet to course. Deer are plenty in the woods, but very wild.

August the 10th At noon. I started this morning down the creek that I lay on last night, but finding that it turned a southwestern course, I resolved to cross it, which I did without much difficulty. It is a large creek and the swamp is nearly half a mile wide. I am now apprehensive that the creek and river I mentioned on the [date illegible] is no part of the Black Warrior, but makes into the Tombigbee west of the Black Warrior, and if so, it may be a great ways to the Black Warrior; yet on the creek I came down yesterday, there is some level land, but it is thin. The growth is red oak, post oak, dogwood, pine and chestnut. There are some good springs, but off from the creek. The land is hilly and broken. As the ground is getting more rocky than it was for some distance back, I am in hopes that I am not far from the river. I continue a southeast course, though slow, for I can hardly get my mare along, her legs are so sore and her back is also hurt. Agreeably to my suspicion at noon, I came in the evening to a large creek, but it does not afford much water now. In about two miles I came to a smaller one, but it did not run. I am now camped on the east or rather south of the latter, and I believe on as good up land as I saw since I left Tennessee valley or rather better. I intend, if nothing prevents, to continue my course in the morning in order to strike the road from Ditto's Landing to the Falls, if these water courses do run into the Black Warrior, otherwise, to strike that river.

August the 11th Noon. I crossed another large creek this morning. These all fun [word illegible]. I then crossed over some very high knobs or mountains. I then came to a branch running nearly south. I came down it so far I expect from the appearance that I have another creek to cross shortly. I have seen no good land since morning, except in the creek bottom, where I had to cut my way with my tomahawk through a canebrake. I continued down the branch to a creek where I had to cut my way through another cane brake, in doing which I narrowly escaped being bit by a large rattlesnake. I then with difficulty got to the top of a very high knob and went a mile and then camped. I saw no good land except in the swamp and that overflows in high waters.

August the 12th I came over some broken ground and high knobs. I came through some pretty good land, if it was level and had water, but springs are scarce—in fact, I saw none. I mean to take a more south course this evening in order to get out of the hills. I came over some high knobs a south course and am camped on a branch that runs south. I expect to keep down to the mouth, in case it keeps that course. I am considerably uneasy on account of some bad looking sores that have been coming on my crippled foot for several days past. There is scarcely any getting out of these branches. The hills are steep and high. I had a rain to-day and it is yet cloudy. I fear there will be more to-night. I wish it might be clear to-morrow, otherwise I doubt I shall stear badly.

August the 13th I started this morning a south course in order to avoid some hills. I have crossed one stout creek twice to-day. It runs nearly south, I intend now to leave it to the right, and bear a little east of south. I have seen no good land to-day that was tendable. I saw some good springs, but the land about them was poor. I kept nearly a south course till late in the evening when I was obliged to turn eastwardly to avoid some impassable bluffs. I saw no good land this evening except one small spot. The ground on it was black oak, chestnut, pine and some poplar. I have gone up some very steep bluffs or knobs and gone down as many. They are here chiefly confined to the water courses and are so steep that I have frequently to put down my hands to assist myself up. I have to wet the soles of my shoes before I attempt to go either up or down, for I have to walk and lead the mare. I have some times been afraid that I and the mare both would slip and tumble to the bottom.

August the 14th I have been obliged to keep considerably to the east this day on account of some very high bluffs and have just crossed a large creek that runs a little to the west of south. There is some good land in the bottom which appears tolerably extensive in some places. I came down it some distance, but saw no chance for water; but the creek is also confined by very high bluffs. I was obliged to rest several times in coming up. I also got some falls. It is very tedious travelling here, for I cannot keep the creek bottom for the cane or bluffs putting in, nor can I keep down the creek or the hills, for the drains or branches that put in on each side are as difficult to pass as the creek. There is but one way to go with any kind of ease, and that is to keep the dividing ridge between the water courses when they run the course you want to go. This way is also attended with difficulties, for if I do not exactly keep the right ridge, I am then involved in drains and bluffs. My foot continues to be very sore. I have made a very sorry out this evening at travelling. In attempting to go more, lost, I got involved in an old hurricane, that has not been burned these several years, and it was so thick with bushes, vines and briers that I was obliged to resume my south course again which led me across another creek that runs into the one I crossed in the forenoon. I am now camped on the bank of this large creek. The bed of this creek appears to be about thirty yards wide, but it does not run enough at this time to drive a grist mill. The bottom above here is not so wide as it was. There might, I think, be got one or two springs in the bank of the creek that makes in above here, but the bottom at this place is rather too narrow for a plantation. I killed another large rattlesnake to-day—ticks of all kinds wonderful here. There was some middling land on the knob, but it is inconvenient to water, and not much of it tendable. I have seen no place since I started that I would like to live at.

August the 15th 1816. I started this morning intending to keep down the creek, but finding difficulties, I resolved to try the knob again, which I did until I came to a branch that runs into the river.[6] I saw no good land nor springs of any sort.

The river at this place is about one hundred yards wide. I would like to cross it, if I could find a place that I could ford. I intend to try this evening, and if I cannot, I will, I believe, go into Jones' valley and try to get some corn, for the mare is nearly done out. I have kept up the river this evening in hopes to find a place to cross, but have not. I made one attempt, but it failed, and I was under the necessity of turning back when I was nearly half way cross, for fear the mare would get her leg broke among the rocks. The river at the place I attempted to cross was, I suppose, nearly two hundred yards wide. The water was very dead. I could hardly perceive it run. The river affords no bottom land of consequence, nor have I seen any spring.

Noon. August the 16th I continue to keep up the river in hopes to find a place that I can cross. It is hard getting along for the cane and briers that are between the bluff and the river; if they continue so long, I will be obliged to take the knob again.

The land in the river bottom, when there is any of consequence, is very rich. I passed through a piece of ground that appears to have been cultivated a great many years ago. It was tolerably rich, but broken.

This river seems well stocked with fish. I have been obliged to quit the river and take to the knob. I will be under the disagreeable necessity of keeping up the river until I can either find inhabitants or a path that crosses. I am heartily tired of this side of the Black Warrior. I saw no good land except a strip about thirty yards wide on the bank of the river, nor any springs except one small one that comes out of the hill in the drain.

I came up from the river in the water—had a disagreeable taste, but the deer appear to resort to it, for the paths lead to it in many directions. I have had a little rain since I stopped and expect more to-night, for it is very thick and cloudy—it is also very warm.

---

6 It is conjectured that this point was between the mouths of Black Water and Lost Creeks, and nearer the latter.

August the 17th At noon. I concluded this morning to return home and for that purpose took a northwest course, keeping the dividing ridge between the water courses, but I have some how missed it and have again got upon a branch that runs nearly north. I mean to follow it to the mouth if it keeps that course.

Water is very scarce here. What I do get is not fit to drink, if it could be avoided. I have not had as bad road and have come much better speed than I have done for several days past. But I dread the lack of water, especially after I get on the mountain, in case I keep this course. I have suffered to-day and am obliged to camp without any.

August 18th Noon. It was misty and cloudy this morning, so that I could not see the sun until it was two or three hours high. I started but stopped again, expecting that I was out of my course. I found after the sun shone that I had gone out of the way.

I have turned a little to the east of north in hopes of finding a path that goes from Milton's Bluff[7] to the Black Warrior, as I doubt it will be difficult getting across the mountain without a path. I have just crossed a creek that affords some good bottom land. The up land is also middling good. It is not very level, but it is tendable. I saw no spring on it, nor do I believe there is any convenient to it. The wood is very thick with bushes, not having been burnt in a long time; it is so [word illegible] horse's traveling.

I have had a severe time this evening with bushes, knobs and bluffs. The mare seems considerably worsted. I came to this creek some distance below, but I could not get across for the bluffs. I again took the knob until I came to a branch that runs north. I took it down to the mouth, and then crossed a large creek, but it runs very little at this time.

As I saw a good deal of sign of deer, I resolved to try and get one in the morning, as I have been three days without meat. At the place I first came to this creek there was a new dam made across it by the beavers. The bushes and briers have made my shins almost as sore as the mare's.

August the 19th 1816. I left my camp this morning in order to try to kill a deer. I had not gone over a quarter of a mile before I saw two fawns. I killed one and have spent the forenoon and part of the afternoon in

---

7 This is a high bluff on the Tennessee river in Lawrence Co. and at the head of Muscle Shoals. In 1819 the town of Marathon was laid out at this point, but it failed to realize the hopes of its projectors and in a few years disappeared from the maps. It is conjectured that this "path" may have become in after years the basis of the old Cheatham road from Moulton to Tuscaloosa.

baking bread and barbecuing the meat. There is a trail that goes up this creek. I mean to take it if it goes any thing nigh my course, and if I can keep it. If it was not for that I would stay here to-night and make boots for the mare out of the deer skin.

I took the trail that led me into a tolerably plain path. It appears to go northeast and southwest. I took the northeast and intend to follow it until I get a more suitable one. I saw one spring to-day, which is the first I have seen for many days. There is also some good land not far from it, but it is broken.

August the 20th 1816. I have got very much deceived in my expectations, for the path has led me almost a south course, and as I do not like to take the woods again, I mean to follow it, if I can, until it crosses the Black Warrior, or until I can find a more suitable path. I have seen no good land to-day of consequence, nor any spring. The range is not very good either.

I came this evening to some Indian cabins that appear not to have been inhabited these four or five years. They are situated on the north fork of the Black Warrior.[8] The land seems to be good but not very extensive. The situation is handsome. Some person has made a little improvement and engraved the letters A. P. on one of the trees. I then crossed below the fork where I got some good spring water. There is also some good land convenient to that, but it is narrow. I then recrossed the south fork and camped. My path continues yet to go too much to the south.

---

8 This was probably a part of what is known on all the old maps as Old Warrior Town, as no other Indian Village was situated in such a locality as is here described. Although Col. John Coffee burned this town in Oct., 1813, it is not unlikely that some of the Indian cabins escaped destruction.—Pickett's Alabama, vol. ii. p. 293. The Indians had a crossing place at Squaw Shoals below the main forks of the river and there were probably a few Indian huts there, but this point is too far South to correspond with other topographical features, principally the entrance to Jones' Valley, the points there passed, and the distance from the falls. Mr. Henry McCalley in his Report on the Warrior Coal Field (1886), pp. 153-4, says:
"Squire Jack Phillips, now of a ripe old age, whose house stands on the site of the ancient Indian Village of 'Old Warrior Town,' says that Black Warrior Chief of the Cherokees, lived in that village, some 50 years ago."
After leaving the vicinity his route run East and then South, which brought him into the Valley in the upper part of Jefferson County.

Early Loyalists To The King Followed Native American Trails To Alabama

During the American Revolution, a number of people who held loyalty to the British cause fled from South Carolina and Georgia, through the dense and pathless forests in Alabama between, to the shores of the Tombigbee River and Mobile Bay. They were the first inhabitants in the counties of Clarke, Washington and Baldwin counties. The only trails they had to follow were made by Native Americans and Carolina and Georgia traders who had been trading with them for years.

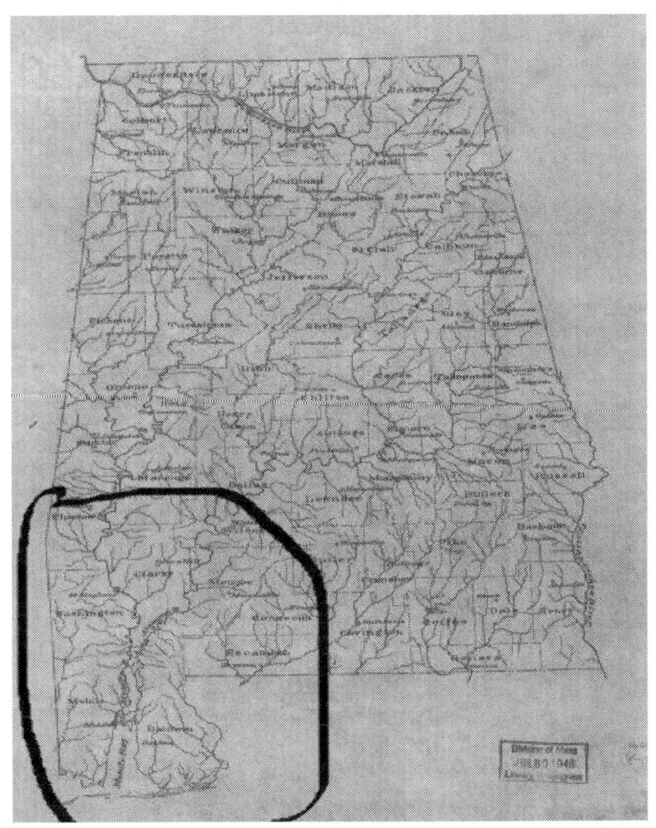

General area of Royalists settlement in Clarke, Baldwin and Washington Counties on 1893 map of Alabama

"As early as 1735 hundreds of pack-horses brought out from Charleston to the Chattahoochie and westward, merchandise for the Indians; and in 1745 Lachlan McGillivray married the beautiful Creek Indian girl, Sehoy

Marchand, and settled with her and established a trading house on the Coosa, four miles above where now stands Wetumpka."

In 1777, Botanist Bartram found a narrow trail for pack-horses from Tensaw up to the Tallapoosa through the thick forests.

Many settlers followed the Native American trails and reached the Tombigbee River before West Florida changed rulers. The Spaniards captured the forts and took possession in 1780, except for the area of Pensacola, Florida which they took early in 1781. In 1783, in January, Great Britain confirmed to Spain, by treaty, all the province of East Florida.

"Great Britain had previously, in the preliminary Treaty of Paris, in 1782, acknowledged the independence of the United States, and recognized the Southern boundary to be the line of 31° north latitude, from the Mississippi river to the Chattahoochie down the Chattahoochie to the mouth of the Flint, from that point east to the St. Mary's river, and down that river to the sea.

A conflict of claims of course arose. Spain claimed by conquest and treaty, and held by possession, as far north as 32°28', or all the former British province of West Florida. Thus at the close of the War of the Revolution, when there was existing in the Carolinas an Georgia so much ill-feeling toward the royalist, to whom the Whigs, so called, attributed very much of their suffering, these distant Tombeckbee (Tombigbee) settlements, under Spanish rule, afforded still to the royalists a secure retreat. Many, therefore, came and settled upon Spanish grants, or opened plantations along the river under Spanish rule."

Some of the names of these early settlers before 1791 and the location were they settled were:

Below McIntosh's Bluff:

- Bates

- Lawrence
- Powell

Above on the river:

- Danley
- Wheat
- Johnson
- McGrew
- Hacket
- Freeland
- Talley
- Baker

In 1791 a new company of settlers arrived by way of Tensaw Lake. Some of their names were:

- Thomas Kimbil
- John Barnett
- Robert Sheffield
- Barton Hannon
- Three brothers named Mounger

Other early settlers names include:

- Hall
- Byrne
- Mims
- Killcreas
- Steadham
- Easlie
- Linder[9]

9 Captain John Linder was a native of Switzerland, had been in Charleston as a British surveyor, and was aided by General McGillivray to settle with his family

"The new settlers with their horses had crossed the creeks and the two rivers upon rafts. The horses had brought upon their backs some plows and axes. They found St. Stephens garrisoned by one Spanish company, under the command of Captain Fernando Lisora. The Choctaws called St. Stephens Hobuckintopa. At this time the commandant's residence, the Catholic church and the blockhouse, were good 'frame-work' buildings, made tight with 'clay and plaster.' Cypress bark covered the other houses, some of which were large." Some French farmers who resided on the rivers were living in clay huts while the Americans built pole cabins."

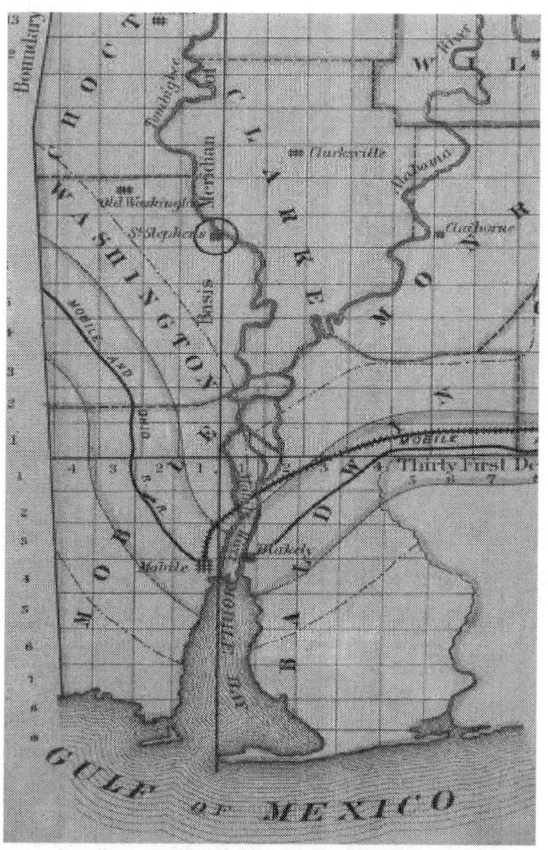

Portion of 1823 map showing Blakeley and St. Stephens in Southeast Alabama

The chief industry was raising indigo which was at the time worth two dollars and a half a pound, a large sum at the time. The Spaniards who lived further down the river were doing a good business burning pine to

and a large number of colored servants at the Tensaw lake during the War of the Revolution. Part of the settlers at this time were royalists and part were whigs.

collect tar.

"St. Stephens, a struggling village of log cabins, was the principal settlement in the Tombigbee region, and here the Government established a post for trading with the Choctaw Indians, and as soon as Georgia gave up her claim to the soil, a land office. "

The act arranging for the disposal of the public domain was passed in 1803 which provided for the validation of claims under the British and Spanish grants; quieted claims under the act of Georgia establishing Bourbon County in 1785; granted tracts of 640 acres to actual settlers at the time of the Spanish evacuation in 1797; and gave preemption rights to settlers occupying land at the time the act was passed."

At the time, settling on public lands was forbidden, but squatters persisted and an act of 1807 extended preemption rights to those who settled in the area. However, future immigrants were again prohibited to coming in and lands that had not already been appropriated were surveyed and put up for public auction. The first sales took place at St. Stephens in 1807.

Early Settlements

Mobile And Louisiana Territory Almost Became An Independent Republic

In 1798, Congress, with the consent of the State of Georgia, organized the territory of Mississippi, comprising the country bounded between thirty-one degrees and thirty-two degrees twenty-eight minutes, and between the Mississippi and Chattahoochee Rivers.

It was stipulated that this organization by Congress was not to impair the rights of Georgia. President Adams appointed Winthrop Sergeant, Governor; John Steele, Secretary; and John Tilton of New Hampshire and Thomas Rodney of Delaware, Judges.

The Natchez District was formed into two counties, Adams and Pickering. The population of this district numbered six thousand. They cultivated the banks of the Mississippi, and the bayous and larger streams flowing into that river. The Chickasaw and other Native American tribes dwelt on these settlements, while the Spanish Government held the country to the south.

The Alabama District was organized into one county, Washington, which owned an area from which twenty counties in Alabama and twelve in Mississippi were later established. The population of the entire territory, excluding Indians, was around ten thousand.

In 1802, the Federal Government acquired from Georgia all of her rights in territory west of the Chattahoochee. It was agreed that Georgia should be paid the sum of one million two hundred and fifty thousand dollars, and the Federal Government stipulated that the Indians should be removed as soon as possible from the territory of Georgia.

In 1801, Napoleon compelled Spain to cede the province of Louisiana to France; but burdened by European possessions and not being able to protect and defend so distant and at that time unprofitable colony, he readily consented, in consideration of fifteen millions of dollars, which was needed by his war camp chest, to cede Louisiana to the United States.

This cession took place April 30, 1803, and at once large numbers of settlers flocked into the territory of Louisiana from many States and established settlements from the Kansas River to the mouth of the Mississippi River. On December 20, 1803, General Wilkinson and the troops of the United States took possession of New Orleans.

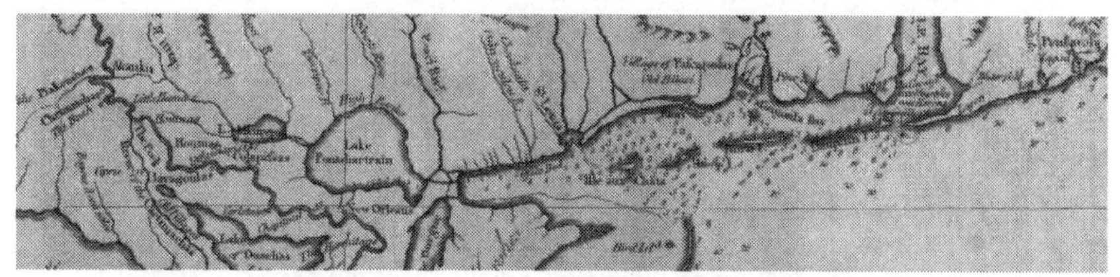

Portion of Map of Louisiana, from d'Anville's atlas 1788

includes Gulf Coastline from New Orleans through Mobile to Pensacola (Library of Congress)

Residents of Spanish garrison and commercial restrictions at Mobile were anxious to occupy the lands around Bayou Sara, Baton Rouge and Manchac on the east bank of the Mississippi and the lands on the Tombigbee and Alabama, south of thirty-one degrees and as far as the gulf, both of which regions fell within the latest Spanish definition of West Florida.

They contended that the cession of Louisiana by Spain to France in 1801 was a cession of that Louisiana of which Bienville had been the founder and which France possessed before 1792, and that when Napoleon ceded all the territory acquired by France from Spain to the United States in 1802 that he ceded not only the region then known as Louisiana, but also that other region extending from Perdido to Bayor Iberville which embraced Mobile, which was once a part of Louisiana, but which afterwards became known as a part of Florida. The United States supported this claim.

Border troubles began to take place between the Americans and the Spaniards. John Randolph, of the Committee on Foreign Relations, even supported a bill in Congress to raise an army to repel the Spaniards, but President Thomas Jefferson exerted his influence and defeated a warlike measure.

However, animosity against the Spanish occupancy grew for several years while the population of Louisiana and Mississippi multiplied.

Finally in August 1810, a band of Americans, calling themselves patriots, and under the lead of the Kempers, who had suffered cruelty at the hands of the Spaniards, organized at St. Francisville, and made a dash upon Baton Rouge and took the place by surprise. Governor Grandpre was killed in the assault. The other posts were captured in succession and the Spanish forces departed for Pensacola.

The territory captured was bounded by thirty-one degrees on the north, Bayor Iberville on the south, the Mississippi on the west and the Pearl River on the east. It embraced the parishes of West and East Feliciana, East Baton Rouge, St. Helena, Livingston, Washington and St. Tammany, in Louisiana, a territory comprising nearly eight thousand square miles and equal in size to the State of Massachusetts.

A Declaration of Independence was published by the patriots and steps were taken to establish a government independent of the United States. The adventure of Aaron Burr, a few years prior to this event, inspired wide-spread ambition to organize new governments after the model of the United States from either unoccupied territory of the United States or from neighboring territory.

The new republic commissioned Reuben Kemper to organize a force upon the Tombigbee to expel the Spaniards from Mobile and all the territory between the Pearl and Perdido Rivers. Many men were organized and moved down the river. They halted one mile above the town of Blakely and sent a note to Governor Folch demanding the surrender of Mobile. While waiting for an answer, they were surprised by a Spanish force and a number were killed and the rest took flight. Some captives were confined five years in Moro Castle. The United States, not wanting to be involved in a war against Spain, frowned on the actions of the Kempers and sent a force to Mobile to protect the Spaniards.

The failure of the expedition against Mobile resulted in a relinquishment of all plans for an independent republic upon Lake Pontchartrain and in the annexation of that region to Louisiana.

Spain continued to hold the country south of thirty-one degrees and to shut the Americans from the gulf, but the United States made valuable acquisitions of territory in other directions.

Huntsville Was Built Around A Great Spring

In 1790, when North Carolina ceded the lands west of the Allegheny Mountains to William Blount, the newly appointed governor of the territory appointed John Hunt captain of the militia. His principal duties were to keep peace in the new territory.

"Everyone living in the territory had heard stories about the new, rich land lying across the Clinch River. This was Native American land and supposedly protected from settlement by the treaties with the federal government. Many families, ignoring the treaties, began to move into the new lands."

John Hunt carved out a respectable homestead out of the wilderness when he learned in 1797 that President John Adams had sent 800 federal troops to evict the settlers. In an attempt to stall his eviction, and probably using his title of Captain in the Tennessee State Militia to help his cause, he wrote the newly elected governor, John Sevier, asking for help.

"Yours of yesterday I am honored with and am sincerely sorry for your embarrassed situation, and would I, to God, I had it in my power to render you relief. You may assure yourself that everything will be done for you that is possible for me, but it is in the president's own power to do whatever he may think best on this very important and alarming occasion. I hope in three or four weeks to hear from Congress and whether or not anything is likely to be done in your favor. In the meantime, I earnestly beg the people, for their own interest, to conduct themselves in a peaceable, orderly, and prudent mannter."

Shortly afterwards, the squatters' claims were recognized." By 1801, the land John Hunt had settled became part of Claiborne County.

John Hunt is considered the founder of Huntsville, but there had been other settlers in the area prior to 1804 when John Hunt arrived. Two of these were brothers Joseph and Isaac Criner, who had built a cabin near the Mountain Fork of the Flint River.

The following excerpt from *The Mystery of John Hunt* By Tom Carney, Editor "Old Huntsville" tells about John Hunt's discovering the big spring.

In September 1804, it is said that, "John Hunt and Andrew Bean left their cabin in East Tennessee and struck out into the wilds on foot, They traveled in a southwestward direction, guided only by the sun and the stars. Almost a month later they arrived at the stream of water now known as Beads Creek, at a spot near where Salem, Tennessee, now stands. At that place they made camp for several days in order to make observations and investigate the surrounding country. According to legend, it also became necessary to replenish the larder. Their unerring rifles soon procured several bear and fat deer, the choice parts of which were jerked and packed for future use.

According to later accounts given by Criner, Hunt and Bean spent the night and inquired about land further south. It was at this time that Hunt first heard of the big spring. The next morning, Mrs. Criner made bread for their journey and the men left to seek out the big spring.

John Hunt and Andrew Bean were not the first white persons to reach the spring. Earlier, in 1802, John Ditto had built a crude shack there and camped for a short while before moving southward to the Tennessee River, where he opened a trading post.

When Hunt arrived, he found the beginnings of a cabin that Samuel Davis had started. Unfortunately, Davis, in his haste to return to Georgia for his family, left the cabin unfinished and when he returned found Hunt had completed the cabin and was living in it. The cabin was a rough one-room affair. People searching for it today will find only a parking lot across from the present day Huntsville Utilities.

The original settlement of Huntsville included many rude log cabins that were scattered along the table lands from Pope's Hill to the big spring.

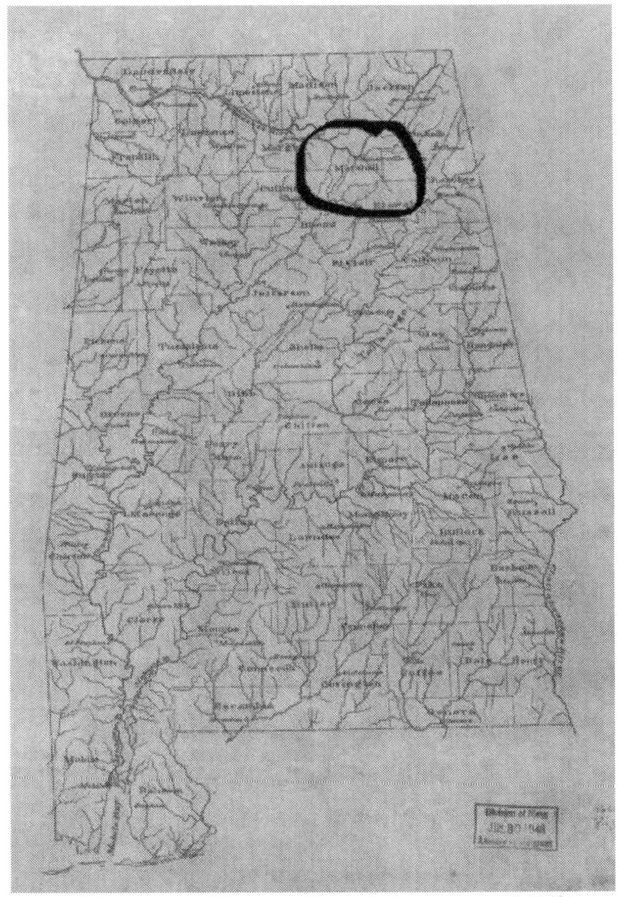

Area of the city of Huntsville in 1893 map of Alabama

(Library of Congress)

In 1806, the United States Government acquired a small triangle of land lying between the Tennessee border and the great bend in the Tennessee River. In 1809 this tract which was the area of the original Madison County was offered for sale and readily taken up by cotton planters from Georgia. Here Huntsville was built about a great spring, and soon came to be the commercial center of the new region.

The following description of early Huntsville is by Judge Thomas Jones Taylor and has been transcribed from The Alabama Historical Quarterly

Alexander Gilbreath had a trading-house or store near the spring, about the corner of Gates and Henry streets. He appears to have been the first merchant in the new settlement, and after the city was laid out he and James White went into partnership and did a large business about the year 1811-12.

A rough country road came in from Holmes street through a mirypond near Struve's corner, wound around the rough knoll, now the Public Square, climbed a steep hill east of the Square and worked its way round to Gilbreath's store and then went down Madison street. There was a path cut out and blazed a mile or two northward, and one going west towards George Dilworth's, beyond Russell's Hill. A sinuous mountain ridge covered with a heavy growth of cedar came nearly to Lincoln street. The beautiful table land along Williams street, where the wealthier citizens afterwards bought large lots outside of the corporation and erected fine buildings, was a fine grove of huge oak and poplar; along Maiden Lane was a low valley, south of which were rough cliffs with caverns and sink holes at their base. The first lot in the new town was sold on the 4th of July, 1810, and the first court-house was commenced soon afterwards. The court-house was sufficiently advanced for holding court in the Fall of 1811, and was finally finished under a contract with John H. Hickman in the year 1816.

By this contract he agreed for the sum of six hundred and fifty dollars to finish the inside wood work of the court-rooms, to paint and renovate the windows and cupalo, and on the latter to place on rods a large gilded ball surmounted by an eagle with outstretched wings not less than two feet across, and there was proviso that if the commissioners of public buildings concluded to have an eagle of copper Hickman was to have extra pay for procuring and putting up same. The old wooden jail stood northeast from the court-house in corner of the Square, and its site is probably outside of the railing. The pond beyond it sometime spread its waters under the jail, and this circumstance caused it to be removed to its present site.

The market was first attached to the court-house, either in its basement or in stalls adjoining, and was first removed to the Holding square, where it remained until the lot on which the market-house now stands was purchased.

The roads leading northward were the only outlets to older settlements; the paths south, west and east extended a few miles to the outer settlements, and ended in narrow trails going into the Indian territory.

The old settlers' cabins were scattered irregularly from Pope's Hill down to Madison street, but there were no buildings erected fronting the public square until after the sale of the town lots. John Brown purchased fifty feet front on Exchange Row and erected two store houses, the first erected on that side of the Square, on the site of the store-houses occupied now by Duncan & Rand and Scruggs, Matthews & Co. James O. Crump also built a house on the ground occupied by the eastern portion of the Donegan block, separated from Brown's house by an alley ten feet wide. Neal B. Rose and Pope and Hickman built the first stores on the east side of the public square, and the first hotel erected on the Square was built by Clayton Talbot.

John Read had been a clerk in the land office at Nashville, but came here in 1810; he purchased the half-acre lot including the west half of Commercial Row and also the lot at Schaudies's corner. He invested extensively in town property, and at one time owned nearly all the land south of Williams street, between Franklin, and a continuation of Green street southwardly to Pagan's creek. He was a prosperous and popular merchant for nearly half a century, retiring from business about the year 1856.

The first house he built was at Schaudies's corner, which he sold to Andrew Jamison who kept a hotel there, which passed at an early date to Allen Cooper who lived there for many years. Among the earlier merchants who purchased lots from Read on Commercial Row and put up store-houses, were Joshua Falconer, James Clemens and Stephen Ewing, and Taylor & Foote.

Stephen Neal, one of the earliest settlers and sheriff of the county from 1809 to 1822, purchased the lot embracing the east end of Commercial Row and sold it to different parties, who built store-houses there. Among these were Luther and Calvin Morgan at the corner, Clement C. Clay, whose law-office fronted on Franklin street, William Patton and Andrew Beirne, long and favorably known to our people under the firm name of Patton & Beinte. They purchased one-half of the front of Neal's lot, were eminently prosperous in business and accumulated large property in the county. Samuel Hazard and William and Andrew Veitch carried on an extensive business, but finally sold out and transferred their business to Philadelphia and Hartford, their native cities.

Among the old hotel-keepers in the city were Christopher Cheatham on Huntsville Hotel square and Archibald Maderra on the Callahan lot, now Chris McDonald's; which last establishment was the headquarters of the convention of 1819, where they frequently met and where they had their committee rooms. When Christopher Cheatham erected his hotel no street was open from the Square to Gallatin street, and he needed an alley ten-feet wide on the south side of the hotel square, to which Col. Pope added forty feet when he sold the lots around the spring. This street, fifty feet wide, was called Pendleton Row a name which it seems, was forgotten or changed and should be restored.

The beautiful level table land gently descending westward from Lincoln to Madison and south of Williams street, just south of the original city limits, early attracted the attention of citizens seeking large lots on which to build their more pretentious homesteads. East of Lincoln street and north of Maiden Lane John K. Lile and Richard Pryor bought lots, on which they settled. Elijah Boardman bought twenty-seven acres of land extending from the Matthew's residence on both sides of Adams avenue beyond Fagan's creek; C. C. Clay purchased the lot where W. B. Leedy now lives; Jno. M. Taylor and afterwards Gov. Thomas Bibb owned the Beirne homestead; Henry Minor the Fletcher homestead, and John Read the lots westward and southward to Franklin street and to the creek.

Pope's first gin-house was immediately in the rear of the Beirne homestead. While much of the city property frequently changed hands, the property owned by Dr. David Moore forim an exception. He came here in 1809, rapidly accumulated property and made judicious investments. Besides his vast landed estate in this and adjoining counties, he owned valuable city property. Land was his favorite investment, and while he bought large farms he seldom speculated in or sold real estate; a large portion of his land was purchased at the land sales in 1809, and afterwards, still remaining in possession of his descendants to the present time.

South of the tier of lots below Williams street Leroy Pope cleared the first farm on his purchase, running south to the quarter section line and north to Pope Hill. David Moore cleared several hundred acres on the Rhett place and built his old brick residence on Whitesburg Pike that stood until just before the war. On his town property north of Holmes street between Meridian Pike and Washington street, he built the first ginhouse in the city and also put up a horse-mill just north of the oaks in the triangle between Meridian and Washington streets. He built a fine residence on Holmes street, which was destroyed by the great fire.

John and William Badlum had a bake-shop and flour-store east of Madison street opposite the junction of Williams, and as far as I can ascertain they put up the first water mill adjoining the city near Clinton street, near where Adam Hall's mill stood. James Barclay, who was Hunter Keel's (sic) partner in erecting the water-works in 1823, built a mill on the Pulaski road where Henderson Brandon's mill now stands.

Leroy Pope deeded to Willis Pope the land west of Whitesburg turnpike in section one, from the township line to the Rhett plantation, and he first located on the Davis Grove property. As far as I can ascertain I have given the location of some of the early settlers in the city from the year 1810 to 1815, at which latter date the city built up very rapidly. The town did not grow much until the year 1815. Although the agricultural interests of the country flourished, yet the times were unpropitious for commerce and trade that build up cities and towns. European wars had ruined foreign commerce, and then came the war of 1812 that paralyzed business for three years. Our people were remote from the scene of actual warfare and did not feel the calamities of invasion, but it interfered seriously with the trade in and cultivation of cotton, and there was but little money in circulation.

After the close of the war of 1812 cotton culture was rapidly developed and our people entered upon a career of unexampled prosperity. The fall of Napoleon gave peace to Europe and new life to commerce. Cotton was in great demand and brought a high price, and the fresh, fertile lands of the Tennessee valley produced enormous crops of the staple. I have given John W. Walker's statement regarding the crop in the year 1817, and it had risen to that amount from the year 1815, after peace was made.

Thomas and William Brandon, the builders of the city, had come here in 1810 with no property except their trowels and great skill in their trade, and from a straggling wooden village they made a city of stone and brick. The court-house was finished but before it was completed there were elegant brick buildings erected on all sides of the Public Square and not less than thirty merchants in business in the city, and a large number of elegant residences completed or in progress of erection in all parts of the city. At the time of the State Convention, in 1819, Huntsville was the metropolis of the State, and had such a reputation that in spite of its locality the idea was seriously entertained of making it the capital of the State.

The survey and sale and occupation of the Tennessee valley lands in the southeast portion of the county, in the year 1818, added largely to the prosperity of the city. The lands offered for sale that year were the finest in the State, and our people who had knowledge of the immense profit in the cultivation of cotton on such lands were ready to buy at ruinously extravagant prices. The value of real estate in the city and county had rapidly increased, and by the year 1818-19 reached its maximum. Real estate reached a point of valuation far above any price attained prior or subsequent to that date. In the year 1818 the county line was extended to its present western limit, and this year was the date of the first settlement of the county around Triana and Madison.

Burnt Corn, Alabama Older than the United States

The first engagement between the pioneer settlers in the southern part of what is now Alabama and the hostile Creek Indians which brought about the Creek Indian War of 1813-14 occurred July 27, 1813, near Burnt Corn Creek, in the northern part of the present Escambia County.

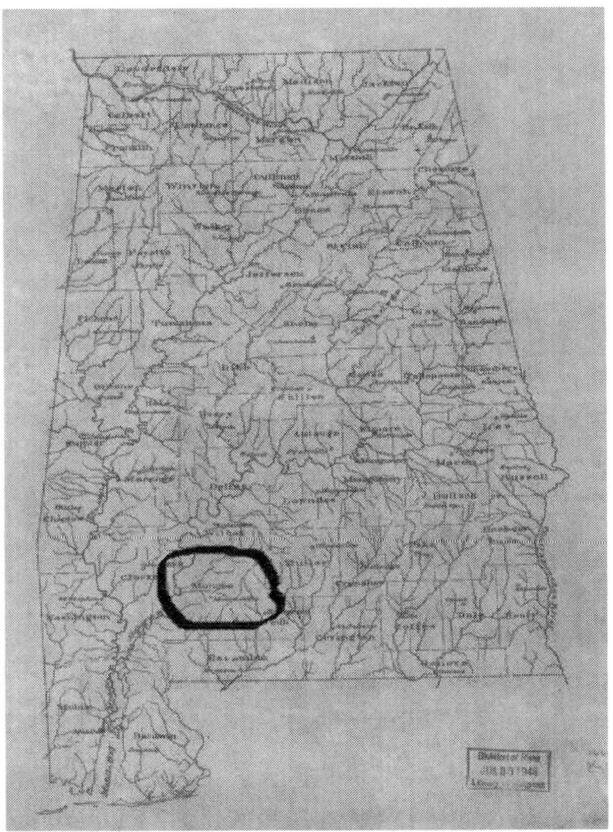

Area of town of Burnt Corn on 1893 map of Alabama

Burnt Corn Creek is a creek in the northern part of Escambia County and a tributary to the Conecuh River. The name is derived from a "large spring, which bursts from beneath the hill below the village" of the same name. The spring is situated on the old Pensacola trail, and was a noted camping round during early Native American times.

No one really knows how old Burnt Corn Creek was named. However, many historians claim that Whites, Blacks and Native Americans were living in harmony in Burnt Corn for almost a century before the fall of 1811 with good trade relations, intermarriage, and reliable treaties. If this true, Burnt Corn was founded sometime in the early 1700's and is older than the United States as an independent county.

There was almost full assimilation among those living in the area. "Among the mixed blood families were these names: Weatherford, Hightower. Tait, Durant, McGilbray (McGillivray). Many were families of high descent among the Wind Clan of the Creeks; they were of the elite of the great Creeks."[10]

Here are four stories that have been circulated from time to time regarding the unusual name of Burnt Corn.

1. The Creek Indians burned the white settlers corncribs trying to drive them on off tribal land.
2. The White Settlers is said have burned the Creek Indians corn fields to claim the Creek Indians land.
3. It is reported that a group of Indians traveling on a path were forced to leave an ailing companion there. They provided him with a supply of corn. When he recovered, he had no way to carry the leftover corn so it stayed on the ground and eventually burned in his campfire. Other travelers came along the trail and noted that they camped at a spring where the "corn had been burnt." The name Burnt Corn has remained there ever since.
4. A party of Indians on their way to Pensacola, stopped at James Cornell's' trading house, burned his corncribs, took his new wife, and brought her to Pensacola where she was traded for an Indian blanket, The creek where Cornell's settled took the name "Burnt Corn" because of the destruction of Cornell's' barn and his supply of corn.

In the fall of 1811, the great Shawnee Chief Tecumseh came to Burnt Corn to incite the Creeks against the whites. He gave a speech at Tuckabatchee, challenging the Creeks to regain their former glory.

Near the spring, also known as Burnt Corn, in the early years of the

10 The Battle of Burnt Corn
http://homepages.rootsweb.ancestry.com/~cmamcrk4/crkwr2.html

nineteenth century, lived the noted Creek Native American, James Cornells. He was the source for the story that the name was given because of the finding of a pile of charred or burned corn at the spring, left there by a sick Indian. Near the crossing of the creek and the old Pensacola trail, July 27, 1813, the Burnt Corn fight, the first engagement of the Creek Indian War of 1813-14, took place.

Prior to the battle, the Creeks had become increasingly concerned about the rising number of white settlers and traders traveling the recently completed Federal Road to the Mississippi Territory. In the early summer of 1813, large numbers of disaffected Creeks assembled at the Holy Ground on the Alabama River. In July, about 300 warriors left the place, under the command of Peter McQueen, Jim Boy, and Josiah Francis, for Pensacola. There they expected to secure ammunition for the impending war from the Spanish governor.

On the way some hostile acts were committed. The hostile Creeks were called Red Sticks because of the red-painted clubs that they carried. Though they had Creek ancestry, the plantations of Sam Moniac and James Cornells were burned and James Cornell's wife was kidnapped. She was later ransomed in Pensacola.

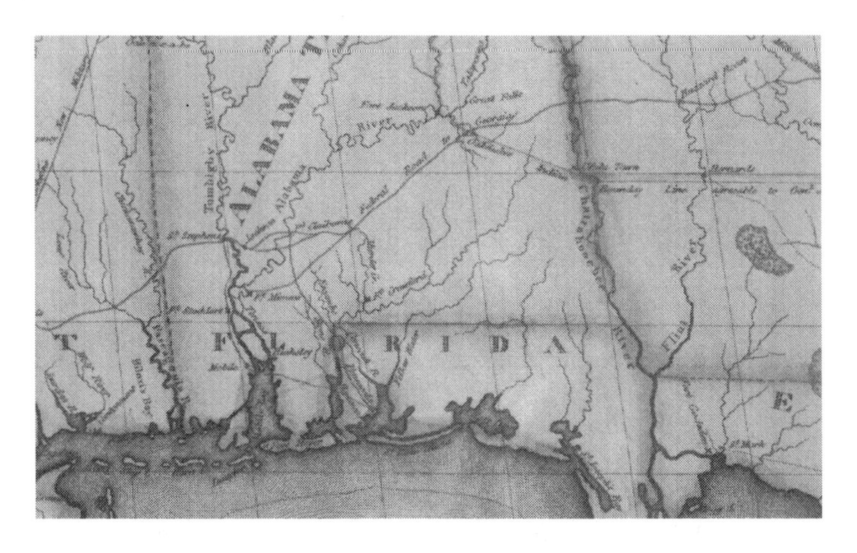

1819 map by John L. Narstin shows Federal road across Alabama St. Stephens, Washington County, Alabama to Georgia (Library of Congress)

It was subsequently learned, through spies, that the Native Americans had procured 300 pounds of powder and a quantity of lead from Gov. Manique.

When the information reached the Tombigbee settlements, Col. James Caller, senior militia officer of Washington County, at once organized an expedition to intercept the Creeks on their return to the nation. At the head of three small companies, Col. Caller crossed the Tombigbee, July 25, and on his march across Clarke County and beyond the Alabama, he received reinforcements, so that finally "his entire command numbered about 180 men, composed of white men, half-breeds, and friendly Indians. On the night of July 26, he camped near the present Bellville, and the next morning took the line of march down the, Pensacola trail to intercept the Creeks on their return."

"The militia group included a company raised and commanded by frontiersman Samuel Dale. The force proceeded eastward from Washington County, traveling part of the distance on the Federal Road, crossed the Alabama River on July 26, and reached Burnt Corn Creek on the morning of July 27. "Scouts ranging ahead of force reported that the Red Stick band was enjoying a noon-day meal at a bend in the creek, called the *Old Wolf Path* and was unaware of the approaching militia."

The surprised Red Sticks were driven into the nearby brush. At this point, it was reported that Caller's men, believed the Creeks were routed and began to loot the camp and lead away the pack horses. However, the Red Sticks returned and mounted a fierce counterattack. Caller's men fell back to a nearby hill. But a "small band of militia members, led by Captain Samuel Dale, Dixon Bailey, and Benjamin Smoot, stood its ground and thus prevented the disordered retreat from becoming a complete rout. Having left their horses unattended, the militia members fled on foot or mounted the nearest horses, including the pack animals. The Red Sticks pursued the men for a short way but were unable to overtake them. Caller and one of his officers became lost in the swampy woods and were rescued about two weeks later, malnourished and delirious.[11] Alexander Hollinger, son of Adam Hollinger and Marie

11 Encyclopedia of Alabama
http://www.encyclopediaofalabama.org/face/Article.jsp?id=h-3081

Joseph Juzan was among the wounded at Burnt Corn.[12]

The militia's casualties included two dead and 10 to 15 wounded while the Red Sticks were reported to have lost 10 men. The militia managed to take much of the shot and powder from the Creeks.

"Reportedly, all of the men who took part in the battle immediately mustered out of the militia, and those who were identified as participants were subjected to public ridicule for many years afterward."[13]

The consequence of the attack was a retaliatory raid on Fort Mims August 30, 1813 which triggered the outbreak of the Creek War. Many of the hostile Creek Indians wounded at Fort Mims died at Burnt Corn Spring.

Another account of the Battle of Burnt Corn by John Simpson Graham in his book, *History of Clarke County* published in 1923 by Birmingham Printing Company, Birmingham, Alabama follows:

BATTLE OF BURNT CORN ARRIVAL

OF GEN. CLAIBORNE'S ARMY

Peter McQueen, at the head of the Tallase warriors; High-Head Jim, with the Autaugas; and Josiah Francis, with the Alabamas, numbering in all three hundred and fifty, departed for Pensacola with many pack-horses. On their way they beat and drove off all the Native Americans who not take the war talk. The brutal McQueen beat an unoffending white trader within an inch of his life, and carried the wife of Curnells, the government interpreter, a prisoner to Pensacola. The village of Hatchechubba was reduced to ashes.

The inhabitants of the Tombigby and the Tensaw had constantly petitioned the governor for an army to repel the Creeks, whose attacks

12 The Battle of Burnt Corn
http://homepages.rootsweb.ancestry.com/~cmamcrk4/crkwr2.html

13 Encyclopedia of Alabama
http://www.encyclopediaofalabama.org/face/Article.jsp?id=h-3081

they hourly expected. But General Flournoy, who had succeeded Wilkinson in command, refused to send any of the regular or volunteer troops. The British fleet was seen off the coast, from which supplies, arms, ammunition and Indian emissaries were sent to Pensacola and other Spanish ports in Florida. Everything foreboded the extermination of the Americans in Alabama. They were the most isolated and defenceless people imaginable. Determined, however, to protect themselves to the best of their means and abilities, they first sent spies to Pensacola to watch the movements of the Indians under McQueen. The spies returned with the report that the British agents were distributing ample munitions of war to the Indians.

Colonel James Caller ordered out the militia, some of whom soon rallied to his standard in the character of minute volunteers. He marched across the Tombigby, passed through the town of Jackson, and by the new fort upon the eastern line of Clarke, and from thence to Sisemore's Ferry, upon the Alabama, where, on the western bank, he bivouacked for the night. The object of the expedition was to attack the Native Americans as they were returning from Pensacola.

The next morning Caller began the crossing of the river to the east side, which was effected by swimming the horses by the side of the canoes. It occupied much of the early part of the day. When all were over the march was resumed in a southeastern direction to the cow-pens of David Tait , where a halt was made. Here Caller was reinforced by a company from Tensaw Lake and Little River, under the command of Dixon Bailey, a half-breed Creek, a native of the town of Auttose, who had been educated at Philadelphia under the provisions of the treaty of New York of 1790. Bailey was a man of fine appearance, unimpeachable integrity, and a strong mind. His courage and energy were not surpassed by those of any other man.

The whole expedition under Caller now consisted of one hundred and eighty men, in small companies. Two of these were from St. Stephens, one of which was commanded by Captain Bailey Heard, and the other by Captain Benjamin Smoot and Lieutenant Patrick May. A company, from the county of Washington, was commanded by Captain David Cartwright. In passing through Clarke County, Caller had been reinforced by a company under Captain Samuel Dale and Lieutenant Girard W. Creagh.

Some men had also joined him, commanded by William McGrew, Robert Caller, and William Bradberry.

The troops of the little party were mounted upon good frontier horses, and provided with rifles and shotguns of various sizes and descriptions. Leaving the cow-pens Caller marched until he reached the wolf-trail, where he bivouacked for the last night. The main route to Pensacola was now before them.

In the morning, the command was reorganized by the election of Zachariah Phillips, McFarlin, Wood, and Jourdan, to the rank of major, and William McGrew Lieutenant-colonel. This unusual number of field officers was made to satisfy military aspirations. While on the march, the spy company returned rapidly, about 11 o'clock in the forenoon, and reported that McQueen's party were encamped a few miles in advance, and were engaged in cooking and eating. A consultation of officers terminated in the decision to attack the Indians by surprise. The command was thrown into three divisions. Captain Smoot in front of the right, Captain Bailey in front of the centre, and Captain Dale in front of the left.

The Native Americans occupied a peninsula of low pine barren, formed by the windings of Burnt Corn Creek. Some gently rising heights overlooked this tongue of land, down which Caller charged upon them. Although taken by surprise, the Native Americans repelled the assault for a few minutes, and then gave way, retreating to the creek. A portion of the Americans bravely pursued them to the water, while others remained behind, engaged in the less laudable enterprise of capturing the Indian pack-horses.

Caller acted with bravery, but, unfortunately, ordered a retreat to the high lands, where he intended to take a strong position. Seeing those in advance retreating from the swamp, about one hundred of the command, who had been occupied, as we have stated, in securing Indian effects, now precipitately fled, in great confusion and terror, but, in the midst of their dismay, held on to the plunder, driving the horses before them. Colonel Caller, Captain Bailey, and other officers, endeavored to rally them in vain. The Indians rushed forth from the swamp, with exulting yells, and attacked about eighty Americans, who remained at the foot of the hill. A severe fight ensued, and the whites, now commanded by Captain S. Dale, Bailey and Smoot, fought with laudable courage, exposed to a galling fire, in open woods, while McQueen and his warriors were protected by thick reeds. The latter, however, discharged their pieces very unskillfully. Captain Dale received a large ball in the breast, which, glancing around a rib, came out at his back. He continued to fight as long as the battle lasted.

At length, abandoned by two-thirds of the command, while the enemy had the advantage of position, the Americans resolved to retreat, which they did in great disorder. Many had lost their horses, for they had dismounted when the attack was made, and now ran in all directions to secure them or get up behind others. Many actually ran off on foot.

After all these had left the field three young men were found still fighting by themselves on one side of the peninsula, and keeping at bay some who were concealed in the cane. They were Lieutenant Patrick May of North Carolina, now of Greene County, Alabama, a descendant of a brave revolutionary family; a private named Ambrose Miles and Lieutenant Girard W. Creagh, of South Carolina. A warrior presented his tall form. May and the savage discharged their guns at each other. The Indian fell dead in the cane; his fire, however, had shattered the Lieutenant's piece near the lock.

Resolving also to retreat, these intrepid young men made a rush for their horses, when Creagh, brought to the ground by the effects of a wound which he received in the hip, cried out, 'Save me, Lieutenant, or I am gone!' May instantly raised him up, bore him off on his back and placed him in the saddle, while Miles held the bridle reins. A rapid retreat saved their lives. Reaching the top of the hill they saw Lieutenant Bradberry, a young lawyer of North Carolina, bleeding with his wounds, and endeavoring to rally some of his men. The Indians, reaching the body of poor Ballard, took off his scalp in full view, which so incensed his friend Glass that he advanced and fired the last gun upon them.

The retreat was continued all night in the most irregular manner, and the train was lined, from one end to the other, with small squads, and sometimes one man by himself. The wounded traveled slowly, and often stopped to rest. It was afterward ascertained that only two Americans were killed and fifteen wounded.

Such was the battle of Burnt Corn, the first that was fought in the long and bloody Creek War. The Indians retraced their steps to Pensacola for more military supplies. Their number of killed is unknown.

Caller's command never got together again, but mustered themselves out of service, returning to their homes by various routes, after many amusing adventures. Colonel Caller and Major Wood became lost, and wandered on foot in the forest, causing great uneasiness to their friends. When General Claiborne arrived in the country he wrote to Bailey, Tate and McNac, respectable half-breeds, urging them to hunt for these unfortunate men. They were afterward found, starved almost to death and bereft of their senses. They had been missing fifteen days. (The above was from conversations with Dr. Thomas G. Holmes, of Baldwin County, Alabama, the late Colonel Girard W. Creagh of Clarke, and General Patrick May, of Greene, who were in the Burnt Corn expeditionby John Simpson Graham)

General Ferdinand Liegh Claiborne the brother of the ex-Governor of the Mississippi Territory, was born in Sussex County, Virginia, of a family distinguished in that commonwealth from the time of Charles I. On the 21st November, 1793, in his twentieth year, he was appointed an ensign in Wayne's army on the Northwestern frontier. He was in the great battle in which that able commander soon after defeated the Indians, and for his good conduct, was promoted to a lieutenancy.

At the close of the war he was stationed at Richmond and Norfolk, in the recruiting service, and subsequently was ordered to Pittsburg, Forts Washington, Greenville and Detroit, where he remained with the rank of Captain and acting adjutant-general until 1805, when he resigned and removed to Natchez. He was soon afterward a member of the Territorial Legislature, and presided over its deliberations. We have already seen how active he was in arresting Aaron Burr, upon the Mississippi river, at the head of infantry and cavalry.

On the 8th March, 1813, Colonel Claiborne was appointed brigadier-general of volunteers, and was ordered by General Wilkerson to take command of the post of Baton Rouge. In the latter part of July he was ordered by General Flournoy to march with his whole command to Fort Stonnart, and instructed to direct his principal attention to "the defence of Mobile."

On the 30th July, General Claiborne reached Mount Vernon, near the Mobile river, with the rear guard of his army, consisting of seven hundred men, whom he had chiefly sustained by supplies raised by mortgages upon his own estate. (Upon the conclusion of the Creek War General Claiborne returned to Soldier's Retreat, his home, near Natchez, shattered in constitution, from the exposure and hardships of the campaigns, and died suddenly at the close of 1815. The vouchers for the liberal expenditures which he made were lost and his property was sold.)

The quartermaster at Baton Rouge had only provided him with the small sum of two hundred dollars. He obtained, from the most reliable characters upon the eastern frontier, accurate information in regard to the. threatened invasion of the Indians, an account of the unfortunate result of the Burnt Corn expedition, and a written opinion of Judge Toulmin, respecting the critical condition of the country generally. It was found that alarm pervaded the populace. Rumors of the advance of the Indians were rife, and were believed. In Clarke County in the fork of the rivers a chain of rude defenses had hastily been constructed by the citizens, and were filled to overflowing with white people and negroes. One of these was at Gullett's Bluff, upon the Tombigby, another at Easley's Station, and the others at the residences of Sinquefield, Glass, White and Lavier. They were all called forts. Two block-houses were also in a state of completion at St. Stephens.

The first step taken by Claiborne was the distribution of his troops, so as to afford the greatest protection to the inhabitants. He despatched (sic) Colonel Carson, with two hundred men, to the Fork, who arrived at Fort Glass without accident. A few hundred yards from that rude structure he began the construction of Fort Madison. He sent Captain Scott to St. Stephens with a company, which immediately occupied the old Spanish block-house. He employed Major Hinds, with the mounted dragoons,' in scouring the country, while he distributed some of the militia of Washington County for the defence of the stockade. Captain Dent was despatched (sic) to Oaktupa, where he assumed the command of a fort with two block-houses within a mile of the Choctaw line."(MS. papers of General F. L. Claiborne)

It will be noted that numbers of Clarke Countians were in this battle, prominent among them being Sam Dale one of the heroes of the Canoe Fight, and G. W. Creagh, whose descendants, a few at least, still reside in this county.

The Native Americans were somewhat successful in this battle, and were thus led to be more aggressive than they had previously been. In the month following they made an attack on Fort Mims.

Native Americans Owned Farms And Raised Cotton

Modern day misconceptions about the Native American population in Alabama portray them as "war-like, nomadic people living in teepees, wearing buckskins riding horses and wearing elaborate feathered headdresses." An article by Ann Nelson of the *The Tuscaloosa News* on July 4, 1976 states the following:

"Those attributes are false according to local authorities on Indian history and culture in the area this area."

She further states that:

"The Indians of Alabama did not even have horses until settlers began arriving in the early 1800s, and then only a few."

The tribes in central Alabama were basically farmers along the rivers of the Black Warrior, Tombigbee, Tallapoosa and Coosa.

Between the Tombigbee clearings and the settled part of Georgia lay the confederacy of the Creeks extending its boundaries northward well toward the Tennessee line. Adjoining the Creeks on the north lay the territory of the Cherokees, extending eastward into Georgia and northward into Tennessee.

Between the Tombigbee and the settlements upon the lower Mississippi lay the lands of the Choctaws, and northward of them the country of the Chickasaws took in the northwestern corner of the future state of Alabama and extended across western Tennessee.

These Native American tribes were further advanced toward civilization than most of their North American kinsmen, and though the westward migration of the whites was still in its infancy, they saw clearly the problem which confronted them.

They had two alternatives compatible with peace—to perfect themselves in the arts of civilization, so as to compete with the new-comers, or to be driven off the land which had been theirs from generation to generation. There was but one other possibility—to fight.

Home of Chickasaw Chief George Colbert built 1790

(Alabama State Archves)

Already game had become scarce to be relied upon as the only source of food supply and all the Southern Native Americans engaged in a crude method of agriculture. They dwelt in villages with adjacent fields of maize, beans, and melons. Their methods of culture were primitive and they rarely produced more than sufficed for their own needs and the more they resorted to agriculture, the less ground was needed for hunting. This may account for the some of the interest the Government of the United States took in the civilization of the Native American and the acquiring of land.

President Washington appointed Indian agents to each of the different tribes and the agent acted as an intermediary between the Government and the Native Americans. The Native Americans were not allowed to buy whiskey from the whites and the whites were not allowed to live among them except by permission from the agents. Permits were granted to blacksmiths, carpenters, wheelwrights, and other craftsmen who were needed. Native Americans were instructed in crafts and often supplied a large part of the demand for skilled workers.

The Native Americans were encouraged to keep domesticated animals and a few of them came to own large herds. They were also instructed in the use of the plow and furnished with seed for planting. The culture of cotton was introduced and they were taught to use the spinning wheel and the loom. Some of the Native Americans learned to make the wheels and looms and turned them out in large numbers.

The Cherokees most readily took to the ways of civilization. They wished to adjust themselves to the inevitable, and through education and industry tried to fit themselves for citizenship. They took up agriculture so seriously that some of them quit their villages for the purpose of living upon their farms. They kept large numbers of domesticated animals, and learned to spin and weave. They built roads and erected saw mills and cotton gins. Sequoyah, a native Cherokee, invented an alphabet so his people could learn to read and write.

The Cherokees even drew up a constitution and instituted a representative government. A census of 1825 shows them, with a population of fifteen thousand and they owned thirteen hundred slaves, twenty-two thousand cattle, over seven hundred looms, more than two thousand spinning wheels, nearly three thousand plows, ten saw mills, thirty-one grist mills, eight cotton gins, eighteen ferries, and eighteen schools.

The Chickasaws and Choctaws, though somewhat less advanced than the Cherokees, followed their policy of absorbing what civilization they could, and remained friendly with the whites. The Creeks, on the contrary, were warlike and not inclined to adapt themselves to the new situation. The strength of their confederacy and the fact that their lands bordered upon Spanish Florida may help to explain their relatively independent attitude.

Just before the War of 1812 broke out, and Tecumseh undertook to unite all the western Native Americans against the United States, he visited the Creeks at one of their great councils, and the younger warriors were incited to hostility against the whites. Though the older chiefs remained peaceful, the war or *Red Stick Party* was powerful and took matters into its own hands.

General Andrew Jackson began his military fray with the Creek Indians and the strength of the Creek Indians, and eventually the strength of Choctaws, Cherokees and Chickasaws was broken by the Battle of Horseshoe Bend.

When the Indian Removal Act was finalized in 1829 and Indians were voluntarily, and involuntarily removed from their ancestral homes, their life as farmers in Alabama was forever gone.

"By 1832 the Trail of Tears was begun and many Indians died on their way west, far from the Alabama forests and rivers." The life stories of those who remained are clouded because the Native Americans who stayed in Alabama were forced to disguise themselves as members of another race. "Memories of their lives and deaths are even darkened with poor information and doubtful historical reenactments of their lives."

Today in Alabama, many of our railroads and highways follow the trails made by the Native Americans of long ago. U. S. Highways 29 and 31 from Montgomery to Pensacola follows the old Wolf Trail. The Native Americans also left many place names throughout Alabama. However, "traces of their language, culture and day-to-day activities suffused into Alabama history."

Land Fraud In Tennessee Led Many To Alabama

In 1782, in an attempt to supply the requested number of troops for defense of the newly independent states, the North Carolina General Assembly passed an act allowing soldiers bounty land at the completion of their military service.

Large land tracts of land in Tennessee were held in reserve to be given to NC Revolutionary War veterans for their service in 1789. However, the land granted to the Veterans in Tennessee was of little use to veterans until they were surveyed and since Indians were living on the land and the land had not been purchased from the Native Americans, the new owners had difficulty claiming their grants. Often, they just sold their land grants to speculators at a low price.

By 1796, Andrew Jackson, a young Congressman at the time in Tennessee, discovered some suspicious business taking place in the Nashville surveyor's office regarding these land grants which led to revelation of a massive Land Fraud, later termed the Glasgow Land Fraud, that implicated leaders in both the State Houses in Tennessee and North Carolina, especially James Glasgow who was Secretary of State of North Carolina from 1777 to 1798.

The investigation in 1797-98, initiated by Andrew Jackson's discovery, also revealed that deeds were executed for dead veterans for more land than service records justified. The invalid deeds were then sold to unsuspecting buyers at a good profit to the sellers.

These same unscrupulous speculators found commanders in the Revolutionary War after plying the commander with liquor to the point of inebriation; the speculators pulled in a willing participant and had the commanders sign an affidavit that the willing participant served in the Revolution under his command. This allowed the now declared veteran to receive an illegal grant which the speculator immediately bought for little money. A few speculators acquired large tracts of land this way then would sell portions of the land to unsuspecting buyers moving into

Tennessee.

When this fraud was discovered by Andrew Jackson, a commission was set up to investigate and validate the deeds. They had so much trouble sorting through the transaction records that they finally decided that the only way validate a deed was to follow the chain of ownership. If a qualified Revolutionary War veteran was not listed in the chain then the last owner lost the property even if he could prove he purchased it legally. Many families were innocent victims from the fraud and lost there property in the process.

The commission involved in validating the deeds was under constant threat and there were at least two plans thwarted to burn the State House where the documents were located as revealed in the incident described below that occurred on January 1798.

On January 18th, men accused in the conspiracy attempted to break into the State House and destroy the records. At night, between the hours of nine and ten o'clock, three men broke into the comptroller's office and carried off a trunk that was said to be the property of William Terrell. The thieves also threw a large chest belonging to Glasgow from the window.

Peter Bird, a slave of Treasurer John Haywood, came by the capitol during the robbery. He confronted the robbers, but they replied only by throwing bricks and stones. Fearing for his life, Bird fled and quickly notified a group of men celebrating the second marriage of Treasurer Haywood at Mr. Cassos' inn at the corner of Fayetteville and Morgan Streets. The men quickly returned to the State House, and the robbers fled. Phil, or Phillimon, a slave of William Terrell, was the only perpetrator caught, and both Terrell's trunk and Glasgow's chest were recovered.

After a trial in the Wake County courts in which Phil was found guilty, Governor Ashe consulted the council of state to determine if the sentence should be executed. Ashe hoped that Phil would admit the name of his accomplices. The council, however, felt that the sentence should be carried through and Phil was hanged. After this attempt to destroy the records, Governor Ashe ordered the hiring of a guard to protect the State House and the commission constantly moved to secret locations to continue their work.

To assist in the prosecution of the accused, the General Assembly passed a court law in December 1799 that created a special tribunal to try the men. In June 1800, five of the twenty-one men originally accused of fraud came to trial. Of those tried, only three, James Glasgow, Willoughby Williams, and John Bonds, were ever found guilty. Having accomplished the goal for which it was created, the court continued in existence for the remainder of its original two year commission.

When the court law expired in 1801, it was extended for three additional years and named the Court of Conference. Next, in 1804, the court became a permanent court of record. In 1805 it was renamed the Supreme Court of North Carolina. Additional changes to the court's structure and composition occurred in 1806 with the addition of another judge, and in 1810 with the creation of the office of Chief Justice. Finally, in 1818, in an attempt to correct all the problems in the existing judicial system, the Supreme Court was established as an independent body.

Trouble with the Native Americans in Tennessee and North Carolina as well as the Land Fraud problems may well have been the reasons many people traveled south to Alabama.

BIBLIOGRAPHY

1. Bancroft's *History of the United States*

2. Archaeological Survey of the Old Federal Road in Alabama by Raven M. Christopher and Gregory A. Waselkov

3. Ball, Rev. T. H. *The Great Southeast or Clarke County and its Surroundings,* pub. 1882

4. Brewer, Willis *Alabama, Her History, Resource, War Record and Public Men: from 1540 to 1872*, 1872

5. Du Bose, Joel Campbell *Sketches of Alabama History,* 1901

6. Publications of the Alabama Historical Society. Miscellaneous Collections, Volume 1

7. Pickett, Albert James *History of Alabama and incidentally of Mississpipi and Georgia,* 1896; Mississippi Dept. of Archives

8. Hamilton, *Mobile of the five flags* (1913), pp. 130, 190, 211;

9. Hamilton, *Colonial Mobile* (1910), pp. 217, 252, 255, 266, 309, 412, 478.

10. Saunders, Col James Edmonds *Early Settlers of Alabama Notes and Genealogies, 1899*

11. Hooper, J. J, editor, *Woodward's Reminiscenses; A Personal Account of the Creek Nation in Georgia and Alabama,* by General Thomas S. Woodward, Published: Montgomery, Ala.; Barrett & Wimbish, Book and General Job Printers, 1859

12. Jeffrey, Reginald W. *The History of the Thirteen Colonies of North America 1497-1763* Methuenn & Co. 36 Essex Street W. C. London, 1908

13. *History of Coosa County, Alabama Chapter One* By Rev. George E. Brewer

14. *The History of Alabama For Use in Schools by William Garrot Brown*, by University Publishing Co., New York. Copyright 1899

15. *Publications of the Alabama State Department of Archives and History:* Historical and patriotic societies series, Issue 6, 1922

16. Library of Congress Maps

17. Fred A. Olds, *An Angel has Fallen'---Story of James Glasgow* in The Orphans' Friend and Masonic Journal. vol. XLIX, No. 11 (July 25, 1924), 1,9.

Dear Reader,

As an author, I love feedback. I enjoy sharing stories about Alabama's history with you. You are the reason that I write.

I need to ask a favor. Reviews can be tough to come by these days. You, the reader, have the power to make or break a book. If you're so inclined, I'd greatly appreciate a review or simply a comment about *Alabama Footprints - Settlement* or on any of my books on Amazon.com or Barnes and Noble. I read each one and take them to heart when I write.

You can see all my books on my Author page on Amazon.com at this link.
http://www.amazon.com/Donna-R-Causey/e/B0052HE4S0/

Thank you so much for reading *Alabama Footprints - Settlement* and for spending time with me.

In gratitude,
Donna R. Causey

Read more books of the The Alabama Footprints Series

ALABAMA FOOTPRINTS Exploration

ALABAMA FOOTPRINTS Settlement

More coming soon!

Additional information on Alabama can be found on the websites:

www.alabamapioneers.com

www.daysgoneby.me

Follow on Facebook at:

http://www.facebook.com/alabamapioneers

http://www.facebook.com/daysgonebyme

and

Twitter

http://twitter.com/alabamapioneers

Other nonfiction and fictional books by Donna R. Causey can be found
at
Barnes and Noble
or
Amazon.com

Follow Donna R. Causey on

www.facebook.com/alabamapioneers

www.facebook.com/daysgonebyme

http://www.facebook.com/ribbonoflove

or on

Donna R. Causey's websites

www.alabamapioneers.com

www.daysgoneby.me

Made in the USA
Lexington, KY
23 April 2016